Going from Homeless to CEO

Going from Homeless to CEO

❧

Inspiring insight on winning the war of life challenges from the Canadian female entrepreneur of the year

❧

Rose Cathy Handy

Design: Jack Steiner
Editor: Drew Tapley
Cover stylist: Courtney Forbes courtneyforbes@hotmail.com
Cover photographer: Derek Lang derekphotoguy@gmail.com

Distribution:
Innovative Logistics LLC
575 Prospect Street, Suite 301
Lakewood, NJ 08701

ISBN 978-1-897404-29-4

Table of Contents

CHAPTER 1

*We can't control everything, no matter
how hard we try*   *1*

CHAPTER 2

*Help can be found everywhere if you
would just speak up*   35

CHAPTER 3

*No one can take your pride and dignity
from you but yourself*   44

CHAPTER 4

*Don't get stuck in the "why me?" But
rather focus on the "how do I get out?"*   55

CHAPTER 5

Forgiveness is a decision not a process   68

CHAPTER 6

*Solve one problem at a time and the
courage to love life and yourself will
come back to you*   79

CHAPTER 7

Using faith to push forward 88

CHAPTER 8

*Setting up a residual income can be
easier than you think* 107

CHAPTER 9

Making success possible no matter what 111

Dedication

To my beloved sweet little sister Esther Handy who passed on while I was writing this book. The pain, the sorrow and the emptiness I feel every day are beyond words. Through you I have learned the true meaning of unconditional love; with you I learned patience, endearment and what it really means to care. You'll forever stay in my heart.

I pray every day that God grants you peace. I am grateful for everything you told me. I am thankful you won't go through pain anymore.

My beautiful angels Estelle Gabbie and Evanna Pearl, you are always why I have the strength to stand through it all. Your love, hugs and kisses remind me all the time that life is truly beautiful no matter what because I can come home and smile with you two.

My mother, my dear mom, it breaks my heart all the time that I can't see you every day. But you have to know that I carry you with me everywhere I go. Thank you for living your life with such grace, dignity and truth.

My dad, wherever you are, I know you are the only person who understands and believes that I always do the best I can under every circumstance. Thank you for everything you stood for.

Acknowledgements

This book could have been a homage to the shelters everywhere for what they do or provide to women in limbo or distress. I am who I am today because a shelter took me in. This is my chance to thank that particular shelter and all the workers in shelters all over the world.

I want to thank all my brothers: Sam, Jean Paul, Augustin and Pascal. Growing up with you guys was the best thing that happened to me. You taught me to fight my own battles and to trust my strength. But you also let me rely on you whenever I needed to. Although I have missed you all the time, and I hate living far away from you all, I hope you are proud of me. Look, I am still standing on my own.

I want to thank all my sisters for being who you are. Even though you guys can be a real pain most of the time, I wouldn't change a thing about you. Thank you for all the times you have been there for me in any way. It meant the world to me. I wouldn't be here without those moments.

I want to thank all the people I have worked with and all my friends. You have impacted my life in a way you will never know.

I want to thank Mr & Mrs Okameme. Sometimes in life, people get a guardian angel. You guys have been my backbone for the past eight years. May God fill your lives with more blessings and peace.

My dear friend Lia Grimanis, I am so grateful every day that I know you. Your determination, your courage and your craziness are what I most admire about you. You are a great inspiration for the way you enjoy life and remind everyone around you that life is to be enjoyed. Yes you are nuts, and that is exactly what makes you adorable, generous, compassionate, and a force nobody would want to mess with. Please stay the way you are and a lot more people will remember that joy starts with a smile. I believe in Up With Women because I believe in your ability to make it what it should be. Keep up the amazing work you do for homeless women and children. I am so thankful to know you and call you my friend.

To everyone going through hardship right this moment, thank you for hanging in there and fighting through it all. Tomorrow should come as another day, and a whole new way.

Going from Homeless to CEO

CHAPTER 1

We can't control everything, no matter how hard we try

THINGS DON'T ALWAYS WORK OUT AS WE PLANNED OR AS WE want them to. We have to be ready not to fall apart when everything starts going wrong, and just take it as a test we have to pass. That's the only way we can find the strength to bounce back or to fight back. Easier said than done, I admit. But that's the simple secret that makes us survive the worst in life. Our attitude toward the situation will help us pass the test or fail it. Our preparedness will help us pass the test or fail it. Our definition and understanding of the situation we are facing will help us pass that test or fail it. I believe this because, otherwise, how can I explain that I was working and making enough money to pay for my house and prepare for my child's birth, but ended up homeless and penniless? I have never been one to over-plan everything. Actually, I am well known in my family and my circle of friends as the big risk taker, not that I put myself in harms ways or anything dangerous. But I have been known all my life as the one who will jump first, and figure out how deep the hole was when I finally land.

I was giving birth to my first child. This was my sacred life-changing moment of bringing another human being on earth. The higher calling, the higher purpose of life I had heard so much about, that I had dreamed about since I was a young girl. I always knew what colour the clothes will be, what cologne I will use for my child, what crib I wanted, what robe I will wear at the hospital, what sandals I will wear and how my hair will be styled. I talked about it when I was a kid, then a teenager, then a young woman. I always knew that bringing my first child to life would be so special, and I had been raised to believe that this is the most defining moment in any woman's life. Everything has to be perfect, everything has to be special, and I would have to plan for it.

I had to learn the first and the hardest lesson of how everything doesn't always go according to plan. It's just a way of life that we all know, but for some reason we are always surprised, shocked, traumatized or altered when we are in that moment when it all goes wrong.

All women usually go through their lives knowing their exact menstrual cycle, fertile and infertile periods; so we know exactly when we can conceive if we have a normal cycle. On the other hand, besides abstinence, if we don't want to get pregnant, birth control pills are a powerful tool to prevent unwanted pregnancy. In my big picture, I planned to have my first child at twenty-nine years old, when I would have my Canadian citizenship and I had been back to school to become a lawyer and have my own practice. I wanted to have children, a lot of children some day or at that point; but not at twenty-five, without my citizenship or my permanent residency of Canada, and with my work situation being less than stable, with me actually between jobs. This was not what I had planned.

I had just moved to my first real apartment, so I wouldn't call this a stable life, but I wanted to make it big, and had big dreams and great ambitions. The radio show I started two years before as a freelancer was really picking up well, and I got offered my own spot hosting and producing my own show. This was major to me. Not quite the career plan I had in mind, but I could make something out of this. So as the thoughtful, ambitious and responsible woman that I am, and after discussing the situation and the risks with my boyfriend, we agreed to have some preventive measures in place so I would not get pregnant earlier than I wanted. To make sure that my plans went smoothly, since I had entered a committed relationship and was living with this man, I discussed my situation with my family doctor and got a prescription of birth control pills. I was well into two years of taking my pills, and felt that I had everything under control, enjoying my life with my boyfriend to the fullest, and preparing for my future.

Things were getting clearer and more stable, and I landed a job at a major bank, handling merchant accounts from chain corporations. A week before my twenty-seventh birthday, a few guests were talking at my house about a young woman who just had a baby. It was pointed out that she was on social assistance and receiving welfare cheques. I kept on wondering how someone can put themselves in that position when we all know how you can prevent those involuntary pregnancies. I kept on bringing up the point that we owe it to our children to make sure we are in a favourable position. I kept lecturing them about the responsibility—physical, emotional, financial and social—we all carry, especially us women, to make sure that we meet all the favourable conditions to fall pregnant or decide to bring a new life on this earth. On my birthday, my sister kept telling me how right now might be the perfect time for me to have a child. I felt she had the audacity to ask me what I was waiting for. I simply answered: "And where would I put a kid right now in my life? What would I do for a kid in my life at this point? How would I take care of a child?"

Four months later I was in Montreal prospecting some opportunities and seriously planning to move there so I could combine studying at university and working. But one little problem kept bothering me: This was the fourth month that I had had my periods, and it had lasted more than the usual three days. I made an appointment to see a doctor, who quickly performed a blood test and an ultrasound. He called me the next day to tell me that I probably had a miscarriage that didn't evacuate itself completely, and that's likely why I was having these prolonged periods. He offered to admit me to a hospital so they could properly clean me internally and make sure there was no residue, and avoid all possibility of infection. What a bunch of rubbish, I thought. And he called himself a doctor? First of all, how in the world can I be pregnant while I was taking birth control pills? If I was pregnant, I would have known it. And how can I have a miscarriage just like that without any alarming signs? I decided not to give another thought to all that, and just go back home and see my real family doctor.

Two weeks later, I was in my family doctor's office for the test. I told him the crazy story from a couple of weeks earlier, and I was clearly expecting him to back me up and reassure me right away that the theory is just preposterous. He decided instead to run tests before eliminating the possibility of me having had a miscarriage. Three days later he asked me to come back because he had noticed something in my first results and he would like to confirm the test. He ran a second blood test. The next morning I called to get the final results for my tests, and I heard a loud "CONGRATULATIONS" from the medical secretary who answered the phone. Puzzled, I quickly asked her what she was congratulating me for, and she said, "You are pregnant... and well pregnant!" I angrily interrupted her with something like, "What are you talking about? I told you I am Ms Handy, which file are you reading?" See, this is why doctors usually insist on being the one to deliver news to patients. "Can you put me through to the doctor, please, and stop talking nonsense," I said. Thirty seconds later the doctor was on the phone, confirming that not only was I pregnant, but I was almost five months pregnant. What? How? When? Who? What? "But I had my periods every month. I had been taking birth control pills. How can this be possible?" I asked. The only response my doctor gave was: "If that's the way you feel, then you better come see me quickly because we don't have much time left."

I went to bed that night pondering what his sentence actually meant. Sure enough, I was sitting opposite my physician the next morning to discuss my "situation". Then the whole thing hit me. My reaction to this incredible and unbelievable news might determine the outcome to not only this baby I am carrying, but also the rest of my life.

My panic and shock gave the signal to my physician that I didn't plan this pregnancy and I was not ready for it, and he would have to refer me to a whole series of specialists, starting with a psychiatrist, and then a social worker. Maybe I really needed a psychiatrist for a shock of this magnitude. Where do I begin? All this was going through my mind, and apparently I asked twenty questions in less than two minutes. The physician couldn't determine which one to answer first. I was so irrational, so incoherent, so horrified that I guess the physician got scared. Then he turned around and gave me the wake-up call: "You still have the option of terminating the pregnancy, you know?"

How can that possibly be an option? I thought. What would it mean for me to get rid of this pregnancy that I didn't plan to have at this stage of my life, and go on with my life as planned, have my freedom, enjoy my life the way I wanted to, and keep planning to have a child one day when I am ready mentally, financially, physically and socially. The bottom line was to have a child when I decided that it was time for me to have one. But medically speaking, it could also be a big risk that may leave me scarred emotionally and physically.

The way I looked at things was that this was the kind of situation when God, nature, and everything else seemed to be aligned for the same purpose: to make me have this baby. I don't care how knowledgeable science is in North America—this is the kind of pregnancy where, if you mess with it, like trying to terminate it, you will probably be the one dying at the end. I mean, I had been pregnant for more than four months without knowing it while I was taking birth control pills. I didn't even think for a second that I should touch this pregnancy in terms of terminating it. You have to be out of your mind to even think that for a second. I did what I could do to plan, prevent, and hope for the moment. But I just had to face the reality that I was almost five months pregnant, and I was going to have a baby. "So doctor, tell me instead what I have to do to take care of this right and make sure that everything works well?" I asked. "This wasn't the pregnancy I planned, but this is the pregnancy I got."

Everything looked perfect on paper

I moved quickly into making a lot of adjustments in my lifestyle to ensure that I had the healthiest pregnancy possible. I had only four months left before the baby's arrival. Four months to plan, to organize everything and buy what I needed.

Growing up, I have seen so many cousins, sisters-in-law, and even my own mother give birth. You would think that I had become an expert in handling pregnancy. But at five months pregnant, I quickly found myself drawing a total blank in my mind. I didn't know where to begin and what to do first. So like always in this kind of predicament, I like to dissect my problem into segments, steps or levels of what I have to deal with, and generally classify them as issue number 1, issue number 2, 3, 4.... At this stage, my issue one was: I was very confused about the process, and had limited knowledge. Issue two was: I was overwhelmed with the timing and whether I would be able to prepare myself and be ready. Issue three was: what does the whole prospect represent for my beliefs, my life and my relationship? I decided quickly to prioritize my issues. All of a sudden, looking at the whole thing in terms of priority, issue number three became less important, so I could deal with it quickly and get rid of it or put it out of the way. Issue number two became the most important as it required serious, quick planning and a lot of adjustment.

Having a baby before you are married brings some technical complications of its own. A child from an unmarried woman has to take the woman's last name in my culture. I was raised in a strong religious family where jokes about the Bible were never allowed. The code of honour, dignity and integrity was so ever-present that even when living over six thousand miles away from my family, and even though my father had been dead a long time, I still carried the burden of that code. The weight was constantly on my shoulders not to disappoint, not to be the one to bring that shame and disgrace on the family name. Therefore, whatever I do has an impact and consequences beyond myself and my life. A girl grows up, goes to school. If she meets a man, he better have the intention to marry her. Then they get married before they live together and start having children. That's what is expected of any girl in my home country of Cameroon. The girl who gets pregnant before she is married is a horrible disgrace to the entire family. They won't throw you in jail, they won't beat you up or kill you, but your life will never be the same again. Now, I was that child who should never do wrong; the one everybody is proud to call sister, daughter or cousin. This stigma of an unmarried woman with a baby stayed with me. If things don't work out with this guy

I am with, I thought, who else is ever going to marry me? No one else is going to want me after this. I will forever be sentenced to a single motherhood life. This is how I was raised; this is what I was taught to believe. No matter how much I have learned academically, no matter how much I have seen throughout my travels and my life, my beliefs were firm on this. I know my family has been judging every part of my life.

So here I was at twenty-something, and my first offence was to be living openly with a man without being married. I never got a chance to explain that to my family who kept on pressuring for answers. I was happy in my relationship, but deep down I could never remove the guilt I was feeling every day for living with a man without being married. Intimately, I prayed for forgiveness from God for my obvious sins, but asked him to actually take the fact that we were living together as my commitment to this relationship, and I was not fooling around. I always knew that God understood and forgave me for this.

My boyfriend and I talked about getting married someday, whenever the conditions were right. But now my guilt and my dilemma were suddenly doubled. Now I had to tell them that I was going to have a baby. I needed their support, I needed their blessing, I needed their love. I decided not to take for granted that they would just all be overjoyed for this new addition to the family. The situation may turn into planning a wedding at the same time as I had to plan for the birth of my child. I only had four months ahead of me, and I couldn't deal with all of this. The lingering question was: "What do I do? How do I tell them and avoid any questions?" My mind was going all over the place, and I was getting sidetracked with all these questions.

I have learned in the past that when I am confused, especially when struggling with my beliefs and thoughts, I should talk to my spiritual friend about my dilemma and confusion. It doesn't necessarily have to be my pastor or my priest; just my friend whom I trust. He doesn't tell me what to do with my life; he doesn't judge me or dictate how I should think. He usually just gives me some solid food for thought that often helps me refocus my attention. Surely enough, when I explained what my head was filled with, he just gave me a simple answer: "Read the book of John, chapter 1, verses 12 and 13; and meditate on it." Here is what it says:

"Yet to all who did receive him, to those who believed in his name, he gave the right to become children of God. Children born not of natural descent, nor of human decision or a husband's will, but born of God." John 1:12–13

Then my friend said to me, "If you believe that God is the only one who decides who gets to conceive and when a child comes to this earth, then you should believe that this is God's decision not yours. Therefore you won't have a problem talking to your folks, your own head or anybody else, and you shouldn't have a problem dealing with it all.

Next, I had to deal with how to take care of a pregnancy. This is normally the easiest part:

- I have to eat well-balanced meals with proteins, calcium, fibre and others nutrients necessary for a healthy pregnancy.

- I have to sleep a lot.

- I have to see a doctor.

I saw my sister and my cousins go through pregnancy, and there is a lot that my mother told me. I quickly learned that taking care of a pregnancy is not a simple thing of just eating well and sleeping a lot. This is just generally what we see from the outside.

First I had to understand the different stages of the pregnancy and how it will impact my ability to walk, sit, run, sleep, dance, and do any normal things I do on a daily basis. Then I had to understand the world of vitamins. Being five months pregnant already meant that I was way behind in my vitamin intake.

I found out about the public health service that is available in every municipality to advise and support women who are expecting. I enrolled myself in prenatal courses to learn the a, b and c of delivering a baby.

Yes I was having a baby, but I wasn't alone in this. I had been living with my boyfriend (we will call him Paul) for two years, and this should also be a big moment for him. The adjustment wasn't just mine. We had to go through this together. He was with me and assured me that he would be by my side every step of the way, and that this was his child out of love, so it is his first priority to bring this child right in life. He was working in a communication company, full-time from nine to five. I was working in a financial institution dealing with merchant accounts, and it took me a month before I told the higher power in the company that I was pregnant. I also requested to change my hours of work since my duties didn't involve handling clients or non-stop phone calls. I requested to start at noon and finish at 8 p.m. This would allow me to avoid the rush hours of the morning and afternoon. I could take more time to sleep in the morning and go to work at my own pace. They agreed and granted me my request.

The arrival of a first baby is very expensive. In our case we only had less than four months to do everything. Luckily we were living in a three-bedroom place with plenty of space to accommodate a new baby, a helper, and friends at any time. Since the work hours were already settled with my boss, Paul and I crafted a little plan to help me go smoothly through the remaining four months:

- We have two salaries, so my salary will go toward the rent, the savings account, baby clothes, mommy clothes, and whatever food cravings I have in the middle of the day while at work. His salary will go toward utilities bills, big items for the baby (like a crib), renovation or room decoration, etc.

- He will essentially be the one running major errands since I have to go to work and take care of myself.

- I will walk to work every time I can since my office was a twenty-five minute walk. This will save us money and provide me with the daily exercise I am required to do.

- We will manage the household chores as we see fit according to our mutual schedules.

Everything looked perfect on paper, and everything worked perfectly in appearance. He was leaving the home every morning to go to work at 7.45 a.m. because it required at least an hour to get there. I will wake up around 9 a.m., get ready, have my healthy breakfast and start walking toward my workplace. He would come home around 6 p.m., which is typical for someone working a nine-to-five job. I would come home around 8.30 p.m. He offered to go pay the rent from now on since it required one of us to go in person, and so I shouldn't worry about dragging my big stomach there. I found this very thoughtful of him. So the first time he came to my office at my break, I withdrew the money from the bank machine and handed it to him to go pay the rent. Then he said that it wasted time for him to come all the way to my place of work just to take the money to go run the errands for me. He suggested that it would be easier for him if I just give him the debit card in the morning when he leaves. So we started operating that way. We had a few glitches here and there that didn't seem a big deal at the time. I asked him to go to Zellers for a baby monitor that I saw on a flyer and thought was affordable. I gave him a fifty-dollar bill to get it for me while he would be at that store looking for a crib. He came back without the monitor and without my fifty-dollar bill, and gave me this bizarre explanation of how he ended up going to the east end of the city, and ended up in a different store than the one I sent him to. Then afterwards, he said they were out of stock for the monitor I needed, so instead he put a deposit layaway on a bassinet that he saw and he liked. I asked him, "Since when do you put a deposit on a little item like a bassinet in a department store?" I couldn't even remember layaways on big ticket items like couches, beds or whatever, let alone a small ticket item like the one he was talking about. Two weeks later, I expected him to bring the bassinet as he promised, but instead it was another little story, and the money was gone.

One day we had a silly argument over a thirty-five dollar nightgown that I asked him to get me to take to the hospital with me. He made a big deal out of it, asking why I needed a special robe. Then he gave me this long lecture on, "Who did I think I was: a wife of the minister of finances?" He went on and on about women giving birth every day with nothing special. A few little arguments like that happened, but they were seemingly minor and unrelated. Each time, I completely failed to connect the dots or see a clear pattern right in front of me.

As far as I was concerned, I was focused on the plan we made, and moving forward. I was eating well, never missed a single appointment with my doctor, and attended all my Lamaze classes. I even signed up for a delivery assistance program where a woman would be with me at the hospital every step of the process. This service was offered by a local health centre to all women who wouldn't otherwise have assistance at the hospital. You had to pay a fee to get a woman assigned to you for your delivery. I worked until my due date. Financially, I was on target according to the plan, and I gave Paul the money to pay for everything that was on my list. I had also been putting money in my saving account so I wouldn't have a financial shortage while on maternity leave. The nursery was ready with everything I wanted. I just needed to wait for that moment.

The Sheriff's note

I was three weeks overdue with contractions under five minutes when I got a call from my doctor's office. They notified me that they had registered me for induction at the hospital because they couldn't wait any longer. I was expected there by 3 p.m., and so I paged Paul and left him a voicemail message. I called my sister and let her know that I was leaving for the hospital, and I called a taxi. I grabbed my bag that had been packed for a month, and headed outside to the taxi that was waiting for me. I opened my door, put the bag down, grabbed the keys from my pocket and turned around to lock the door behind me. Then I realized that there was a one-page government document taped on my door. The first question that went through my mind was: Why didn't they knock to give me the paper directly, since I was home? The second thing I realized was that my door seemed to be the only one with that notice. Then I thought that maybe the other people picked up theirs already.

I moved closer to read what the notice was all about. First I saw that it was addressed to me, well no surprise there since I lived at the address, and this was my door. I saw that it was signed by the Sheriff's Office. It said something like: You have been hereby ordered by the Court to vacate this property by such and such date. The Sheriff will come to change the locks at 5 p.m. today. We expect you to be gone and all your belongings removed from the property. Anything left behind will be seized by the Sheriff and you will have to pay a fine to collect them. Reason: failure to pay the rent; you missed the court date; no response to all the attempts to reach you on this matter.

I read it through, but didn't make a big deal out of it as I was firmly convinced that this was a mistake. It had to be, there was no other way. I was paying my rent every month, I didn't receive any notice, and I didn't receive any indication that I had to show up at any court. Who ignores that kind of letter anyway? So this can only be a mistake.

I managed to get into the taxi and go to the hospital. Once I settled into my room, I was on the phone immediately and sent Paul a second voicemail to call me back as there seemed to be a problem. My next call was to the property management office. I told my story about the notice I had found glued to my door earlier, and concluded how it must be a mistake because I gave the money every month for the rent, and my boyfriend comes there every month to pay the rent. I related to the gentleman at the property management office how I was at the hospital right now about to deliver my baby any minute. So I invited him to just pull out my file and look at the records and he will see the proof of everything I was saying. I asked him to please do me a favour and contact the Sheriff's Office and tell them they made a mistake on the name, and I gave him my number at the hospital to call me back. Then I had this silence on the phone for a few seconds. I said, "Hello? Are you still there?" He softly answered that he was listening while looking at my file. Then the life-altering moment came. He started by congratulating me on the baby. Then he said how he sympathized with all that I was going through, but he is sorry to have to tell me that my file has no record of me paying any rent for several months. They have sent a lot of reminders that went unanswered, and that's why they were left with no other choice but to seek an injunction from the court to kick me out of the property. At this stage the only way to stop the proceedings is by paying the amount in full plus the legal costs, but even then he couldn't guarantee that the Sheriff's Office won't go ahead and enforce the court order. But at least with the payment, that can be a good start.

At this stage, my heart is beating so fast my blood pressure went over the roof. I couldn't feel my legs anymore and my stomach was pulling so hard that nobody could tell if it was a real labour pain or just the baby fighting to survive because I was literally suffocating her in my stomach. I was completely into the labour of excruciating grief while trying to hold it together and convince the office clerk that he was making a mistake on the file. He can't be looking at my file and seeing what he is describing, I thought. I started again telling him the long tale in details: what time my boyfriend came this month to get the money at my work; details of what I was wearing, what I was doing the minute he called to let me know he was at the lobby. The little jokes we said to each other that day. I kept talking to him and giving him details as if I wanted time to be my witness and to tell the clerk that they are all making a mistake, because I did pay my rent every single month. He quietly responded that again he really sympathized with what was happening to me. He then suggested that if Paul was coming to pay the rent every month, then he should have the records from receipts. He invited me to ask him to bring them to their office before the end of the day, and by all means they would correct the situation if they made a mistake. But the way he saw it right there and then, was that something was not right and it was not from their records, so I had better get my boyfriend to bring the receipts as quickly as possible. I promised him that it will be done before 6 p.m.

I called Paul again, this time into a 911 mode, which meant

it would ring non-stop until he took the message. I didn't want to wait, so I called the company where he is employed, and I asked to be transferred to the program in which he was working. A supervisor came on the phone and told me that they have no employee with that name in the program. I said, "Please don't joke with me. I am absolutely in no mood for jokes at this moment, and no time to waste either." She said, "It's not a joke. I don't know anybody with that name in the program, and I've been a supervisor here for the past nine months." She suggested I check with another program as maybe he mistakenly gave me the wrong name. I was transferred to another department, but got the exact same response. So I asked to be transferred to the human resources manager, because this is the only place I could have the correct program where he goes to work every morning after he leaves home. Now I was speaking to the HR manager, and I quickly explained the predicament I was in and how urgent it was that I talk to Paul who works there. But they kept telling me that they don't have anybody with that name in any of the programs or departments, which was odd because he left the house every morning with his briefcase, and came home around six as a normal nine-to-five worker. So I asked her if she would kindly check and tell me where in the company he works so I can talk to him and tell him I am at the hospital delivering our baby. I needed for him to have special permission to leave work early and run home, get all the receipts for the rent payments, and take them to the property management office before 6 p.m. Otherwise, I won't have a home to take the baby to after delivery. She promised to help in any way she could as she understood the urgency of the situation. She put me on hold for ten seconds, then came back to deliver the other devastating piece of information: "Yes I have his name on record here, but unfortunately, he was terminated six months ago." This time, it was my head that started spinning, and the only reason I didn't pass out, I guess, is because I was lying down on the bed already, with all the machines hooked up to me monitoring my blood pressure. Somehow I was still trying to believe that once he showed up everything would be all clear, and this would all just be a big misunderstanding. But after that phone conversation with the HR manager, I couldn't be in denial any longer. This was it, I was down. I took a deep breath and said to myself: "I am down but not finished".

Hiding problems

I spent three days in the hospital waiting for the baby to come out. Looking back at the whole ordeal, I always thought that, subconsciously, I didn't want the baby out because I was afraid of what would happen to her. I felt like she was more protected staying in my womb than outside. The nurses kept on coming and going. For three long days, I suffered the pain of the contractions under five minutes, lying down on my bed with all these machines and tubes to control my blood pressure. Sometimes it would get so low, sometimes it would get so high. Nobody could explain what was going on with me. The nurses kept saying how they have never seen anything like this. My sister was coming every day after work and spent the whole night praying in the chapel. Some friends staged praying sessions around the city to cleanse the air and help smooth my delivery. The helper that the health centre sent to assist me was sitting there twenty hours a day with me, telling me story after story just to distract me and help me relax. She ran out of stories to tell. Nobody could explain why a three-week overdue mother-to-be, who had been induced into labour on Wednesday, was still not getting into full labour after three days. I looked healthy, the baby was breathing just fine and looked healthy too, smiling at times and reacting to the contractions, which is normal behaviour. But my blood pressure was running abnormally crazy.

All I wanted was to protect my child. My focus was to protect my child. So I thought that I had to be quiet about all the drama that was unfolding with my housing situation, because if I spoke up, everyone's attention was going to be on the issue. I needed everyone's attention on me delivering a healthy baby. I didn't want this whole thing to become a distraction to the situation. But by doing so, the nurses and everyone around me were steered in the wrong direction, and kept on imagining different hypotheses of why I was still not delivering the baby. They were trying all kinds of things to help, because they were there to help and wanted desperately to help, but they just didn't know what to do. So they wasted three days doing the wrong things because the problems they thought they were solving were not the real problem. I knew I had to be quiet about Paul turning out to be a horrible nightmare, particularly to this sister of mine sitting right there. She was completely against me going into a relationship with this guy, especially going to live with him. She tried so many ways to stop or discourage our relationship; but like usual, I didn't listen. I focused on the means she was using to prevent me from entering or staying in that relationship, and I never gave her the benefit of the doubt to see beyond and understand or accept what she was observing: that this guy doesn't seem good or right. She reminded me time and time again in her own twisted way how smart I was and that I deserved grand things and the life of a queen in a palace. Now I was in hospital about to end up with a baby by this guy who turned out to be worse than even the lowest thing she was imagining. How could I look at her and tell her she was right, and let her make me feel even dumber than I felt? No way. I can't take the lecture or the "I told you so" silence, or even the pity; not now! But by doing so, I really threw away all the moral and emotional support she was ready to give with no strings attached. On top of everything, she is a professionally trained psychologist. So who can know better than a psychologist what to do in this kind of situation? How to sort through the feelings you are experiencing, the emotions you are going through, the different pains you are handling? Yet I chose to be quiet, thinking that I was protecting my child from the drama, when actually I was protecting my ego more than anything else.

I decided to delay the contractions for as long as I could help it, and I was so convinced that I had some control over the delivery. All I had to do was to be quiet, relaxed, and not accelerate the contractions. Then they started coming under two minutes apart, and I told myself: That's it. Don't go any lower. I am in a hospital, I am safe here. As long as my child is in my womb, she is safe there and well protected. I wanted her to stay there as long as I could manage. I wanted her to be born in a loving home with warmth, laughter, joy and peace; and I envisioned her bouncing in the arms of her loving, caring dad. But that's no longer the dad she might have if she comes out. That's no longer the home she might have if she comes out. That's no longer the life she might have if she comes out. So why put her through that misery, disappointment and pain? She is better off staying inside my womb, at least until I can solve this issue or get it sorted out. I needed to buy some time, just a few days, maybe a week. I was sure something would happen, and I would bring her out then so she could have all that I dreamed for her, all that I wanted for her. She deserved a loving and caring father who would rather die before letting anything happen to his child; a beautiful warm home where she could grow and be all that God intended her to be; a devoted mother who was at peace to nurture her and guide her through life with unconditional love and wisdom. Technically, a woman can't control the labour or delivery. But the mind has power sometimes, more than we give it credit for. I am still convinced that the power of my thinking was a hundred percent the reason why, from Wednesday to Saturday, I didn't go into full labour. They tried everything to force that labour, and nothing happened. But by doing so, I didn't realize that I might be dangerously harming my baby inside more than I was protecting her. I didn't remember that she was already three weeks past due, so the clock was ticking, medically speaking. All sorts of complications can happen that could kill my baby. The baby was not eating properly because for three days all I had was an IV. I was thinking that I was relaxed and everything was fine, but the blood pressure monitor was telling a different story. I was subjecting my baby to the highest level of stress unintentionally, which was extremely dangerous at that point. The fatigue, the trauma, and maybe not enough oxygen—this wasn't good for a baby.

My new mission was to get everyone to leave me alone in that room. Everyone was becoming too persistent in finding out what was wrong with me, and I was so afraid that they would find out. I started being mean to the nurses, the helpers, and everybody else. I made it seem as if they were agitating me, and I started screaming and yelling. Everybody was ordered out of my room. By doing this I had created a whole set of events that put the medical personnel in high alert. And when they panicked, they could make drastic decisions that may carry heavy consequences. They were talking surgery to get the baby out.

There is always that time in life when you know that you can't hide from the problem anymore. You have to face it right on and handle the fallout. It can be a voice of reason that speaks to you, the revenue agency that gives you a call, the collectors that corner you, the hole that just keeps getting deeper and you don't want to go lower. What makes the difference between people who survive their ordeal and those who get swallowed by their problems, is the ability to recognize that moment and have the courage to handle it. This is the moment when you get fear out of your mind, and you choose to start taking a look at the situation itself. It's the moment you make that decision that you only have up to go. In my case, that moment came on the Saturday afternoon. My big sister had had it, and she had a huge argument with Paul outside in the hallway where they were all standing. She demanded to know from him what was bothering me. Of course, he claimed he didn't know. Without knowing the truth, she accused him of being the reason why I was having all these delivery issues. Of course, he denied it. She asked him to explain why my blood pressure went over the roof every time he entered the room, and was convinced that for some reason he was a great source of distress for me. So for that reason, she wanted him out of the entire hospital, and he'd be called when the baby was out. He reluctantly left. Then my sister just barged into my hospital room and said: "I don't care if you don't want anybody here. They are discussing whether to operate on you to get the baby out. I don't understand why you have to go through surgery to have your baby. You are not sick. Listen, I don't know what's going on with you, but it's obvious to me that you are scared of something, and it has nothing to do with the pain of pushing a baby out. I don't care what it is, but stop holding that baby in. The baby has been ready to come out for a long time now, and wants out... so let her out! You are the one who chose to become a mother, and nobody forced you into it. This is it for you. It is time to show yourself and that baby you are holding in there that you can be a mother. And it starts now. Get this baby out, you hear me? Get it out."

Two minutes after that order, a nurse entered my room and started preparing some scissors, surgical knives, and all the rest of the things they need to operate. Then I realized that my sister wasn't kidding, they really wanted to operate on me. Thirty minutes later, I pushed the baby out naturally to protect her from the ordeal of surgery. She was a beautiful, healthy 9.8 lb baby girl. The minute I hugged her, all my fighting spirit came to me, and I knew that the best way to protect her was to start by confronting the problem head on and find solutions. I am her mother, which means I will have to be strong enough for both of us from now on. I will deal with whatever it is that prevents her from having the life I have dreamt for her. I will confront everything for her, and unfortunately, this includes her own father. I can't control everything. I can't control people's behaviour, but I can take care of what I have in my arms, and what I am aware of.

I know that every time we experience hardship, we go through so many different emotions: guilt, disappointment, resentment, shame, anger, abandonment, powerlessness, humiliation… and the list goes on and on. I was no different.

I managed to convince the property management office to talk the Sheriff into giving me an extension of two weeks instead of the forty-eight hours stated on the notice. I decided to use it to deal with this problem.

Confronting the problem

In any situation, there is *a* problem and then there is *the* problem. The more effective way of making sure to clear the mess is to confront the problem itself. There was a problem of losing my house, and I had another problem with my bank account having been emptied. I had been keeping this whole thing to myself, not letting people around me, except the property management office, aware that my life was crumbling when I was supposed to be going through the highest joy of every woman's life: my first baby. All these little issues were different little problems that could be resolved here and there. At this point, you don't need to be a genius to figure out that the whole thing was just masking the real problem. The bigger problem was the one I had to focus on. But when tackling these kinds of situations, it's always important to think about what exactly you are confronting, and avoid building the wrong expectation. I had to dissect the problem itself. I couldn't be blindsided anymore in expecting that Paul would bring my money back. Let's face it, if he had the possibility of having that money somewhere, he would have found it a long time ago and replaced mine that he had stolen. So it would be a waste of time or wishful thinking to sit there and ask him to bring me my money back, or expect him to even have an answer that would solve anything. The same way, it was a waste of time to start asking him why he had lied time and time again about everything. It was no longer the time to think with the heart. The head had to take over because the reality was staring me in the face, and wasn't the time to choose to be blind. The way I saw it was as if my emotions were in an all out war with my will, and the battle I had to win was that he was not going to take me with him mentally, emotionally, physically or socially.

First mentally, I had to detach myself from him. Up to this moment I was looking at him as my boyfriend, someone who was part of me. His pain was my pain, his problem was my problem. If he had flaws or shortcomings, I will complement him and vice versa. But the way he treated me and our whole life clearly showed that he didn't view us the same way. So from now on, why should I keep thinking of us as being one? So I literally took him out of my head and placed him in front of me; but more than that, I saw him as coming against me. I knew I had to protect myself against him or he would swallow me back in, and I couldn't allow myself to be swallowed back in again because

I knew what was in there, and it was not good. Therefore the only option was to see us as two separate people going against each other, and I wouldn't be the one going down. Once this separation was done in my head, then I got the courage to start getting a hold on my emotions.

Stage two was for me to look at my feelings. I trusted the love I felt for Paul, and still believed every loving word I had ever said to him. But then I also acknowledged my other feelings: hurt, anger, betrayal, disgust, disappointment and hate. Whether it was toward him or the situation, it didn't really matter. The important thing was to recognize that I was feeling all that. Knowing that we can't possibly feel all this at the same time for the same person, I came to terms with two boyfriends hidden in the same body. At that moment it didn't even matter which one of the two he was. If he could remotely be the other one that stirred these kinds of feelings in me, then I have been in the wrong place all along. Since I didn't want to be feeling all those negative things in my life, I had to separate myself, and take my love somewhere else. At that moment I was at piece with my heart and my head, and the rest was just how I would take action and which actions I had to take in order to physically remove myself from the whole situation.

Stage three was to deal with the outside and create a stepping stone for me to move on with my head held up high. I already knew that I was going to lose my place, and I didn't even know where I would be going. It's very easy to tell somebody to leave your house and to get out of your life, or that you don't want to see him again. I always thought it should be about more than just asking him to leave the house that he had the gall to stay in, and kept on coming there as if nothing was wrong. We were all going to lose the place anyway. But how convenient for him, that I have been keeping his dirty little secret. Nobody knew what he had put me and my baby through. He was still going around laughing with people, and I was the one carrying the burden of the situation. At the same time, the burden was lifted for him. He was now acting liberated. No need to hide anymore and fake going to work. No need to steal my money behind my back and make up all these stories. If I didn't tell my own sisters what's going on while we were at the hospital, then I was keeping it a secret. So he was free. If we were not together the next day, it would just be that we had separated for whatever reason, but no one would know what he had done, because I have been protecting his image. Well this was war, and we were at the stage of battle. I was not going to let him confine me into this wounded little woman who will have to live with the shame of a failed relationship, a failed household and failed financial health. I was the one carrying this huge burden that was eating me up. I didn't do this to myself, he did this to me. Why was I even protecting his secret? This made me an accomplice to his misdeed as if I condoned his behaviour. I shouldn't be the only person who knew this. I had to speak now, unload myself and free myself, I thought. If anything happened to me or my baby, who's ever going to believe me if no one knew what's going on. A guy who can do this can be capable of anything. I didn't believe that he would harm me physically, but I couldn't be certain of that. Besides, as far as this guy is concerned, I didn't know what to believe anymore. On the other hand, if nobody knows, who's to say that he had any remorse about this whole thing, and that he won't go do this to the next woman he's with. I called all my family members, and all his family members and close friends that had any influence on him, to a meeting at my place. I made it sound like it was because of the baby's arrival, but once the people gathered, then I told them everything that had happened. I openly asked him to leave my place and warned him that if anything happened to me or my baby, they were witnesses. This was a great morale boost, and very liberating.

Stage four was to deal with getting out of the relationship even though we now shared a child. I was new to this maternity thing, and the prospect of raising a child alone is the most terrifying thing that would make anybody vulnerable to the temptation to keep even the person they loathe the most in their life just to have the illusion of help. I didn't have the chance to even enjoy my maternity. We all agreed that the relationship was doomed, and I made it clear that the relationship was irreparable. I told him that it would be best if he went to live somewhere else. I wanted him out before the Sheriff threw me and my baby out. I asked him to take a week to make other arrangements, and leave. Well to my surprise, he quickly agreed to that, but then turned that week into a living hell. From bringing back people and other women to the house as he pleased, to loud music, the slamming of doors, anything and everything. The week went by quickly, and of course he didn't leave. He said he was not going anywhere. Then the threats and accusations started coming. He said he would kill my baby before he would ever let me take her away from him. Since we had lived together for more than two years, this made us common law partners, and therefore he said that he would be seeking financial support from me since he didn't work. I called two different lawyers for advice on the matter, and among a lot of things they both quickly asked me to get the police involved, which I did, immediately. The police in turn advised me that whenever he started the threats again, to just call them and have them take a listen. They instructed me on how I should manage the call, and since we had two separate lines, it was actually easy. His phone line was in the living room, and my line was in the bedroom. So the police instructed me to call them from the bedroom when he started his rants and

Going from Homeless to CEO

threats, and leave the phone active, and they will listen. Once they heard something they could act upon, then they would be there immediately.

Soon enough, it started happening. The first day I was terrified but I managed to do just that. I called the police from the bedroom and left the door open so they were able to hear everything. The second night it was the same thing. The third night I thought it was just unbearable for the police themselves. When I started repeating to him, "Don't come near me, why don't you just go?" there was a knock on the door. The police were there and asked him if he had a place to go. If not, they would find him one, but he had to go. He wanted to gather his stuff, but they told him that it would have to be another time. The problem was solved.

Solving the other little issues

After I had exhausted all my appeals and pleas with the property management office, the legal services, and the women support services in my neighbourhood, I had to come to the painful truth that my baby and I were officially going to become homeless. I was going to be on the streets, and I am forevermore going to be homeless. What a dreadful word!

Until that moment, being homeless meant the guy that I had seen sleeping on the street at night in the middle of snow with just his pile of dirty old blankets to comfort him. This is when he is lucky enough to find a corner of some government building or a coffee shop. Or there are the homeless people that I have seen in movies, talking to rats because they have become the only trusting parties around them. Or worse yet, the ones who had to sleep on top of a sewer lid just to feel some kind of heat generated by the filth underneath, just to stay alive. I pictured myself pushing my baby in a broken grocery shopping cart, probably stolen by some runaway teenagers, going from place to place. Then I imagined that cart becoming my baby's crib, bed, home, and the only stable place she will ever come to know. Yes homelessness was going to become me and my newborn baby.

I thought what a failure I have become. What a horrible way to end up. After all that I went through all these years of my life, after all that I have survived already, this is what I was going to be.

Just one month earlier, I was so excited about life, motherhood, family, possibilities… everything. I was so looking forward to being at home, enjoying my new life of becoming a mother. All that I had seen other women do after they had their babies, now it was my turn. How did I come to this point? Oh God, oh God, what did I do to deserve this? My child whom I love and was looking forward to raising in this beautiful quiet home, with two loving parents, will now forever be a statistic, like those children who don't grow up in stable homes and end up in jail, on the streets, or worse.

At that moment, I screamed to myself, "Just snap out of it," just like I had to say so many times throughout my life when my thoughts start to take me to some dark places, and the prospect is so deeply negative and out of control that I just refuse to go there.

"Yes, snap out of it!" These were just thoughts, and what you do with thoughts is snap out of them, especially if they are negative, destructive, demeaning, and stripping you of all power, or treating you as if you were dead. I was not dead. I was just being evicted from my home for heaven's sake.

Once I shouted that to myself, it was almost like a rebirth. I felt new energy, new strength, and a new will to look at my situation at that particular moment. I was not going to worry about what would happen to me tomorrow, next week, next month or next year—just what was happening right then in that moment, and what I can do about it. That's what I had to focus on first before

I got into solving anything else. Suddenly I was realizing again that I had my head, my arms, my feet, my brain; and I was still breathing. I looked back at the last month and realized that I had done a lot I didn't even know was possible the day I found out I would be out of my home, and that I was out of money. I was able to stay longer inside my home, and my baby was still healthy because I was able to find help to get food. Therefore, all I needed was more support to go through the rest of my little issues.

I had to identify the real little problems, and weigh in the options. I needed a place to stay and to keep eating until I could start getting money again. That's the known big issue. But what exactly did I have to solve? I made a list of my needs. First I had to vacate the place I was staying in, which meant I had to pack my belongings, find a place to store them, then move them to that location or just get rid of them. Then I had to find out how I was going to pay for my living (food, baby stuff, and other necessities). I was entitled to my maternity allowance, but it would take at least eight to twelve weeks for it to start coming. I could go back to work, but then what would I do with the baby? I didn't have my citizenship yet, so I was not entitled to everything, nor did I have access to all the things available out there. I couldn't even dream of a short-term loan. Where can anybody get financial assistance in this city when you are on the street or you don't have a fixed address? What if my baby gets sick? What if I get sick on the street? Who will take care of my baby? What if I fall asleep? Who will keep an eye on my baby? How can I actually avoid ending up on the street? Could I find an apartment somewhere where they will let me live until my allowance starts coming and I will be able to pay for rent? All these thoughts went through my head. So many questions I was facing; and so little time to answer them.

The first person I thought about was my pastor. I went to see him and explained the whole situation. He asked me what was best for me. Since I didn't know how long it might take for me to find a different place to live, and it would be best to have some money just in case, should I sell all my stuff to make some money? He said the church could organize a garage sale for me to sell my things, and offered the second option of storing my belongings in the basement of his church. I jumped on that second option because I was convinced that my situation would be resolved soon. I didn't want to get rid of all my stuff because it cost me my hard-earned money, and I was also thinking that if my homelessness got resolved sooner, I didn't want to be in a situation of buying everything again. So we ended up agreeing on the option of storing my stuff in the basement of the church. But because he couldn't guarantee the safety of the place, since it wasn't a closed room, and people come and go there all the time, he advised me to separate my things, and maybe just store my furniture and kitchen wares. He quickly found me two gentlemen who came to help me pack and separate what could go to the basement of the church and what I needed to store somewhere else. Once that was done, they took the furniture and the rest of the big boxes to the church.

I still had my computer and other things to store somewhere else. So I started asking in my community if someone had a garage, a basement, or a closet where I could put them. After two days, one gentleman offered to not only take the rest of my stuff, but to make space where the computer could be set up so that if I needed to use it anytime when I was feeling better, I can go there during the day and use it. The only problem with that arrangement was that he lived in the east end of the nearby city. It would take me at least two hours to commute to his place if I ever wanted to use the computer, which meant another two hours to go back to wherever I would be staying. So I took him up on his offer to store my belongings, because at least I knew that they would be safely stored there. Since he knew that I had no money to pay for moving, he also made arrangements with some of his friends to come pick them up from my place and move them to his location.

All this was hustled in my last two days before the deadline I was given to vacate the property. So the final D-Day came, along with the big issue of: where do I go to live?

Accepting the fate of homelessness

I had one day to vacate the property, and this time the Sheriff was really coming to change the locks, and was scheduled to be there at five in the afternoon. It can appear surprising to a lot of people that someone will end up on the street, not having anywhere else to go. Yes, you know a lot of people, you have friends, you have family. But the place you end up spending your nights is a box in a corner of a building, or a shelter, or a basement of a church. I had a sister who had a house, but when I asked her, yes she offered for me to go to her place, but with certain living arrangements. She was willing to wait until I start getting my money to collect rent from me, as long as it didn't take more than two months. I would also have to agree to live by her rules. That last part wasn't a big deal because I went through that with her before, and I was paying my rent, paying for my food and doing my part of the chores. The problem was the sleeping arrangements she was offering. There was a couch in the basement of her house that I could sleep on, and there was a small room upstairs that was not big enough to have more than one single bed in it, so she offered to have the crib installed there and have the baby sleep in the crib in that small room on the second level of her two-storey house. Those were the only two available spaces in her house at that point. The idea of me sleeping downstairs on a couch while my newborn baby would be two levels above me was just too terrifying to even imagine. Every time I check on her, I will have to climb two levels of stairs just to get to her. What happens if there is an emergency in the middle of the night? My sister wasn't the type to compromise. There is no negotiation to go with it first and see what adjustments would be possible after awhile. Therefore, I couldn't take that option as it was too scary and more risky than living on the street. At least I will have my baby all the time with me.

I called three people that I thought were friends, but they quickly told me that they didn't have space for a woman and a newborn, especially if I didn't really know how long I was going to need a place to stay. After those three rejections, I stopped calling. I had too much on my mind, and the time was running out on me. I had been warned that if I was not out by five, I would be removed by force and the door would be locked for good. "It's a procedure, nothing personal."

I called all the cheap motels I found in the phone book, and explained my situation, and offered to pay them as soon as I had the money. They all hung up on me. It was 1 p.m. when I started to panic because the street was really coming to me. I thought of persuading the property management officer to give me an extension or at least the flexibility to keep on looking until I found a place to go. Then he asked me if I had tried women's shelters.

I said, "Women's what?" He said, "Shelters". I asked what that was. He explained that a shelter is a place where homeless people go and sleep. Sometimes you might be lucky to find one where you can actually live there. You don't pay rent, but you participate in chores or programs. I asked where I could call, and he gave me a social services office that was two blocks from where I was living at that time. I went there in person, and a gentleman there was kind enough to give me a long list of shelters. Because his working hours were ending mid afternoon, he had to leave, so he handed me the list and encouraged me to keep calling. I called more than fifteen, but: "still no space," "full capacity," "waiting list," "no women allowed"... were the answers I kept getting. In some other places I was getting a voicemail, and I would leave a message with a highlighted urgency: "Please call me back. I am desperate. I don't want to sleep on the street with my new baby. Please, please, please, find me a place in your shelter". I called everywhere and went back to the places where I left messages, hoping to catch a live person. Unfortunately nothing happened.

I figured that there was nothing more I could do at that point. I had to accept the inevitable, and I sat down on the floor and started thinking of the best place where I could ensure safety for my child. It would have to be a place that is clean all the time, a heated place because it was the middle of winter, and a place that is always open, where people circulate, and where there are chairs and benches. My preferred location was the hospital, and I thought that if I went and sat there in the waiting room, no one would bother me or ask me a question. If they asked me a question after awhile, I would just move to another waiting room of a different department. If the hospital doesn't work, then I will go to the bus terminal. It is never closed, and people come and go from there all the time. No one will touch us because there are witnesses, and the place is well heated. My last option was the shopping mall downtown. Once I had that plan down in my head, I said a prayer and headed into the room to dress my baby and hit the streets.

I got so scared that I called my friend again and asked him if I could stay at his place just for one night to get used to the idea that I was going to be on the street. I got a voicemail and left a message. Luckily, that reminded me that delaying it wouldn't change anything. If I had made a decision to go with the street option, the sooner I started, the better it would probably be. Honestly, in the same manner that I was trying to convince myself of that, my head was also telling me that I was not ready to go live on the street. I picked up my baby as I wanted to feed her one last time in this place of ours before we go. Then my phone rang. I knew it wouldn't be the property management officer. Just like a person sitting in the execution chair hopes that the phone call will be a message from the governor, I was hoping that it was my friend, my sister or my pastor calling to say they have changed their minds, and they had reorganized their homes and were able to make some space for me, and I can go stay there. Well it wasn't any of them. Instead, a voice said, "Hello, are you Rose? My name is Christine, and I am calling from Women in Transition. You left a message here earlier. I am sorry no one was available to call you back. We are very busy. We didn't have a place available until this afternoon, but a woman we were expecting did call to cancel her request. So if you are still looking for a place to stay, I called to tell you that we might have one for you."

She wanted to add something, and I didn't want to let here finish, jumping in with, "Yes, yes, yes. I'll take it. I desperately need it," because I didn't want her saying something that might stop my heart that was beating so fast already. I was still holding my baby in an empty room. She said, "That's good, but what I wanted to say was that the place is only available starting at eight, and you will have to be here no later than nine because we have a policy where people don't come in after nine. The other thing is that you have to qualify, so I want you to tell me a little bit about your situation." We spent ten minutes on my story, and I was in.

CHAPTER 2

Help can be found everywhere if you would just speak up

I ENDED UP IN A SHELTER HAVING LOST EVERYTHING. BUT THAT'S not what I was most ashamed of. I kept on thinking how dumb I was. How could I blindly trust someone that much? I mean, this man is just a human being, and every education I had received in life, whether it's academic, social or spiritual, points to the one common fact of human beings as flawed. So why didn't I question things, ask to see receipts, ask for confirmation? Why couldn't I see the signs when they were practically screaming in my face time after time? There were clues, now that I think of it afterwards. He is not a con artist or someone who preys on women. This is a nice guy, clean, well behaved and very considerate. He didn't mind doing the laundry, the cooking, the shopping, the banking, the gardening, the housekeeping... everything. I was the luckiest woman on earth. So how could I question a man like that? How could I question a little incident like one day I had a gold ring that disappeared from the box in our bedroom. Nobody else had access to our bedroom. I knew that two years earlier he told me about pawn stores as we needed a big sum of money to pay off a debt he had. This debt was preventing us from being approved for an application we had submitted. I had a lot of nice jewellery from before, but when we got to that pawn shop they couldn't offer much because it was all costume jewellery. He got so mad that day, and was yelling about how was it that I didn't know the difference between real gold and costume jewellery. How I wasted his time letting him go there hoping to make money out of my jewellery.

But I had that real gold ring. So a year later, when my real gold ring actually disappeared, I didn't connect the dots. I should have known from his insistence on selling our stuff, and his always having a great explanation that I wouldn't question. I had the signs, they were all staring me in the face. Why didn't I take a minute to look at them closely?

My instincts were sometimes telling me that something was not right, but that only lasted a few seconds. The only time I was unsettled with a situation, I remember confiding in my sister about it. Then she told me to stop because she couldn't believe that this guy can do anything wrong. If there is any problem, it has to be me, she said, and went on by saying that everything was going right for me right now, and instead of being grateful and thankful, I wanted to start looking for problems. Well, I thought that maybe I was just exaggerating or my mind was overreacting; so I let it go. One year later, that situation turned out to be that he got a young girl pregnant, the same one he had introduced to me as his niece; the one I gave free access to my home. They would spend so much time on the phone together. She came to our place and I went to work leaving them there. Well she turned out not to be his niece after all—but his mistress.

All these little bits of memories were now just flowing in my mind while I was lying down on my bed at the shelter. I had never felt so ashamed of myself and so humiliated. I felt so unworthy of my daughter that I was holding. How me, the same person who went to university at barely sixteen, with an IQ of over 150 at the time, the one deemed so exceptional that the government awarded me a special scholarship to study political journalism. How me, the same person who had had high profile people like top athletes, business executives, high-ranking public servants, at my feet begging me to be with them, and I ended up like this, in this predicament. How me, a pillar of my community, who sits on the board of directors of big organizations because people value my ideas, my principles and my personality, and respect my behaviour. But then at the same time I can be duped like this? How me, the woman that my parents raised with such high morals? I started talking when I was eight months old, but here, when I should have asked more questions, push the curiosity a little bit deeper, analyze a bit more the answers I was getting... I chose to put trust ahead of common sense and my better judgment.

I couldn't help but think that the whole world was thinking that I was the dumbest woman that ever lived. If I was that clueless and that idiotic, maybe I deserved what I was getting. The world can't be filled with people like me; and to think that I just brought another human being on this earth. What am I going to teach her in life?

I didn't want to show my face out there ever again. From the way things stood, there was no place out there where I could still go and have the respect or the consideration everyone had for me before they found out. I was done, ruined, over, beyond redeemable. No one will ever trust my judgment ever again. No one will ever trust my ideas ever again. And no one will ever respect me again. All those people I rejected because I felt they were beneath me will laugh at me now. Everyone who will look at me from now on will only see: dumb, dumber, and the dumbest woman on earth. I couldn't take this, I couldn't change this, and I couldn't erase this. I couldn't even move away to another country because there was nowhere for me to hide.

Luckily that day I fell asleep. Luckily it was my fourth night at the shelter. Luckily I was alone in my room and in my head.

Your thoughts can make you or break you

The next morning the reality of the day came to me and I knew from the minute I opened my eyes that it was a new day. I felt better, and meditated that morning on: "We are more than conquerors".

The mind is a beautiful place, but it can also be a deadly weapon. Our thoughts can empower us, but they can also poison our lives or kill us.

I have volunteered my story everywhere possible in the hope of inspiring people and changing their minds on homelessness, empowerment, and the importance of communication. My story has inspired people everywhere, and I hope it will continue to do so. When I meet people on the street and they tell me that they read about my story or watched it on TV, I always asked them which part moved them. I want people to be moved by the fact that I dare to come out in public and say it's not a secret, and that this is what I went through, so if you are going through the same ordeal you are not alone. Take comfort in the fact that other people have experience in similar circumstances or events and they are still breathing, laughing, going on with their lives, achieving great things, and moving on with their lives.

My inspiration to share my story shifted the day I watched it air on television. It wasn't my own story that captivated my attention, but the segment right before mine. The segment was about a lady who went through similar circumstances as I did. She had a boyfriend who subjected her to all kinds of humiliation and abuse. She lost everything she had and was living secluded in her house. She was living alone, only going out once a week for groceries, and was so convinced that people were judging her and talking about her that she had to hide. For a while her story was the talk of the town, and it was just too much for her to take. She quit her job. She stopped talking to her friends and neighbours, who used to see her come out once a week. They noticed that they didn't see her anymore, but then they stopped paying attention. They assumed she left town, and that no one lived in her house anymore. They never bothered to care enough to go see her, reach out to her or check up on her. They just focused on their lives and minded their business. When the police finally found her body, it turned out that the whole situation left her so severely depressed that she couldn't come out anymore. She stayed inside her house until she died there alone. It was impossible to establish if she committed suicide or if it was a natural death. Regardless, she was dead, and had been for a while. It took a personal inquiry about her from a different city that led the police to her house.

I was frozen to my chair. The tale was profoundly chilling. Then my story came on that same evening. At the end, only one question stayed in my mind: How can two women go through similar, bad situations, yet one dies and the other survives? The difference lies with how we manage our thoughts and how we relate to the situation. Help is everywhere around us in the form of counselling, assistance, support, listening, and more. The moral of that story for me was to ask people, to speak up. I know it is not easy.

It's your life at stake and nobody else's. This is your survival war

We live sometimes in different environments that don't always allow or encourage us to speak. This is when the art to detach oneself from the different layers of a situation is instrumental in helping manage the thoughts that come flowing in our minds. It's always a lot to sort out. I hate to believe that death is an option for anybody. We have too much at stake, including our own lives. It's actually in this moment, this perfect moment, when we need to be mindful that the battle we are engaged in is one of survival. It's our life that is at stake. So we need to reclaim it back. Pressure is something we deal with every minute of our lives. Sometimes it comes from unthinkable sources, the pressure that makes us stay silent and creates the belief that we are responsible for what is happening to us, and therefore we have to punish ourselves with isolation, seclusion, humiliation and shame. We need to be aware of that risk and make sure to remember all the time that nobody deserves to go through this pressure, and more importantly, you don't deserve it either. If life has chosen for you to endure the hardship, you have to believe that you will ultimately win this battle of survival. You have to find the strength in you somewhere to fight this battle and win it. You can show life that you deserve the other side of it, not this nasty one you are being handed. If you don't see that you are at war against life and condition yourself to win the prize of the right to live the good side of it, that's when everything corners you and it becomes hard to get out.

I had a fiancé the year my story aired for the very first time. The reporter was focusing the story on how I survived a lot in life. I was raped as a student when I was nineteen; and then this abuse by my boyfriend Paul a few years later. My fiancé was someone I knew for a long time, and we were getting along really well. We were making wedding plans, and he knew my story, all the details of my life. He knew them way before I chose to talk to the reporter. So I called him to let him know that I had a long interview with a reporter, and she would be talking about my life very soon. He inquired about the part of my life they were interested in reporting. I told him the whole story, and didn't leave any details out. I explained that my story is about overcoming hardships, surviving no matter what, and having the courage to go on with your life regardless of the struggles or the falls. He asked again if I shared everything, even the molestation and the rape I was a victim of in previous years. When I answered yes, I noticed a pause in the conversation, but didn't know what to make of it.

Soon enough, the story aired. It took him an entire day before he had the courage to call me in reaction to the broadcast on TV. When he ended up calling me at the end of the next day, he accused me of being selfish and self-centered. How inconsiderate of me to tell the whole world about all this, he said. Certain things are best kept to yourself. Do I have any idea what kind of embarrassment I was bringing to my family with this story? He asked me if I realized how much shame he felt, and that he doesn't even know how he will show up at work again because now everyone will look at him as the fiancé of the woman who was abused by some other guy. "Why couldn't I keep my mouth shut about this?" he asked. Most women stay quiet, and of course when it comes to me, it's too much to ask. "Do you know how humiliating it is to know that your woman claims she has been raped? I mean how does a woman get raped anyway? Why didn't you run? Why didn't you scream? Since this was someone who knew you, how can it be called a rape? You probably encouraged him or gave him a sign that you're interested in him, or something else, I don't know. But I am sure you did something that enticed him your way. Now I am forever going to be known as the man with the woman who was raped and homeless. This doesn't sit well with me at all."

Well, first I asked him why he was focusing on only that part anyway? Then I added: "So you want me to keep quiet about my life because it will embarrass you? I can promise you that we won't have a happy and harmonious life if this information stays just between us. Just from what I am hearing you say, I actually feel more compelled to speak up. If there is still one person out there who thinks that a woman is responsible for being raped or abused in any way, then I have to speak up. The silence you are requesting from me is deadly for me, for you, and potentially for us. What will happen when I can't stand being touched anymore by you just because I have been so quiet, and my emotions and thoughts overwhelm me and I can't separate my feelings anymore? What will happen when I turn to heavy drinking, or swallowing pills or other things, just to numb the pain? What will happen when I start choosing to stay inside my house because I have lost touch with reality and can't interact with people outside, and I am overwhelmed with violence inside my head and feel that the only solution for me is to die? What will happen when I turn to violence to deal with everything or communicate with others, and I end up hurting someone that I care about, while nobody understands why I am behaving this way?"

This is what silence could do to me. Silence makes people lose a sense of reality. Silence makes people lose their minds. Silence makes people become alcoholics, drug addicts or abusers of any other deadly substance. Silence makes people become violent and aggressive, therefore running the risk of never breaking the cycle of violence. Silence turns people suicidal. Silence makes people withdraw from life. Who can possibly want that or wish that kind of life for a loved one or for themselves?

As you see, if I want to have a life then I have to speak up. How can anyone suggest silence when your life is at stake? You have lived the horror of the incident alone, and if that wasn't enough, why would someone want you to go on living it alone? Speaking about it is very liberating, therefore your first step toward freedom from this horrible thing is to speak of it and get it out of you. I had to claim my life back, take back my power and control over my own life.

Unfortunately, if you have a problem with that, you have to do what is best for you. I am even going to be blunt and advise strongly that you participate in seminars or workshops to learn more about the issues of coping with abuse victims. You need to educate yourself more on the subject so you learn what it is and how you can better handle the situation if a loved one has been a victim of abuse. I don't blame you if you can't live with the image of knowing everyone around you is aware that your wife or girlfriend was abused. It was also hard for me to be with a man who had a problem with that side of his image. And just like that, the relationship was over.

The temptation is lurking all the time to go back to the same old habits, same old types of people we used to know, that ended up abusing us. People don't want to be alone, and want to have partners. The pool of people we will associate ourselves with is vast, and we just have to be diligent in selecting the people we associate with. Sometimes we make ourselves so vulnerable that we don't see the trap we head into.

You should never keep something bottled up inside just out of fear that someone will leave you. Once you start, you will never be yourself ever again. The power to be you starts with the freedom to think without fear, speak without fear, and live your life without fear.

You have it in you to take it back.

CHAPTER 3

No one can take your pride and dignity from you but yourself

I HAVE LEARNED FROM THE BIBLE THAT "PRIDE GOES BEFORE destruction" (Proverbs 16:18). We are supposed to reject pride because it's a negative thing, a sign of peril, a lead to failure, destruction and fall. But growing up, that's not what I have learned. My dad used to literally hammer us every morning about pride and dignity as if one is a virtue and the other one a reward. Either way he urged us to equip ourselves with these two things always. He would say, "Life will bring a lot of enemies your way, but if you arm yourself with pride and dignity, you will defeat them every time".

The big question is how you keep your pride and your dignity when you have been humiliated to the bone, when you have fallen from grace right to the dirtiest mud, when you have been ridiculed and belittled to the core of your soul. As much as this seems so huge and insurmountable, I always shock people by saying that the answer to that question is as simple as: all you have to do is turn your head the opposite way and turn your body just a little, then move one foot two feet forward, then bring the other one. There you have it, problem solved. It is that simple. You are still you, but the circumstance has changed, the location has changed, the view has changed. Therefore you shouldn't care any longer about the old place you were standing at, even if it was just for a few minutes again. I guarantee that no matter what, wherever you are standing right now is a hundred percent better than where you were a few minutes ago. This is for the simple reason that anytime you are in control of your own body, choices and decisions, you can only choose to place yourself in a better or more favourable position; and you will avoid any complicated, crowded or risky position.

The real question is: Why are we so quick to surrender our pride or dignity whenever one little part of our feelings gets hurt? When someone plays you for a fool, that doesn't mean that you actually are one. But you can quickly become one if you allow it.

There are many ways in life to make sure that your pride and dignity are protected no matter what.

Don't take responsibilities for others' bad behaviours or faults

People are always so quick to take the blame for someone else's bad behaviour. How often we go through simple things like walking on the street and someone is so distracted or in a hurry that they bump you and knock your bags out of your hands. They don't apologize for it, and instead you find yourself claiming that it's your fault, and you should have paid more attention and avoided the person. They leave you there to pick up your things from the floor by yourself, so apologetic that you didn't give the creep enough space to walk without pushing you around, and blaming yourself for what just happened. To top off the whole image, someone is always ready to come and reinforce that idea by saying something like, "Poor thing, are you alright? I saw what happened, it's not fair. Are you going to be okay? Here, let me help you pick up your stuff. Be careful, okay!"

I always tell people that if you are the person that was bumped, at that moment, scream at this person taking pity on you: "Are you kidding me? Don't 'poor thing' me. If you saw what happened then go knock some sense into the creep you saw bumping me. Go tell him or her to be careful. Go talk to him or her, not me."

You can't take the blame when you are at the receiving end of a wrong doing. You can't make yourself responsible for a bad thing that happens to you. It's like you are quietly sitting in your living room and a drunk driver comes crashing into your house; then you turn around and say: "Why was I sitting there?"

From the many interviews I gave about my story, I remember a young reporter who wanted to write about my story because she was preparing a piece around International Women's Day. She said she became interested in interviewing me, and was taken aback by the lack of shame and the humility I was exhibiting. So she wanted to explore this in an interview with me.

I said, "shame? What shame?" I know that when people look at abused women, homeless women, or women who have been victimized—they expect to find them wounded, broken, depressed, vulnerable, and feeling worthless. These are the exact stereotypes I try to get women to avoid locking themselves into. People tend to confuse humility with alienation. I don't. Humility has a biblical and spiritual virtue to me that makes me treat people with respect and makes me thrive to do good and accept that human beings can be flawed sometimes. It can't possibly mean that I have to alienate my self-worth to the shortcomings of someone else.

My self-respect, my dignity and my pride are not for sale

I don't hand them to people for free either. They were instilled in me by my parents, nurtured by my education, shaped by my cultural values and principles, and grounded by my spiritual life of more than twenty years. Why would I surrender them to some-one I have known for less than three years? I know who I am, and I try not to lose sight of it. The father of my child cheated on me, and not the other way around. He lied to me, not the other way around. He stole from me, not the other way around. He is the one with these issues, not me. So anyone who expects me to breakdown and start crawling on my self-pity will wait for a long time, and it will not happen. I refuse to be responsible for someone else's morals, and I refuse to be responsible for some-one else's mistakes. I refuse to be responsible for someone else's bad behaviour. I was at the receiving end of all that, so I choose to be me.

My dearest hope is for a lot of women to remember that and claim their lives back.

Don't lose your fighting spirit in the process

The courage to stay strong is the underlying struggle when you need to overcome obstacles. Contrary to what people believe, I think we all have it in us to fight and overcome challenges and obstacles. Nature will throw a lot at us throughout the course of our lifetime, and we have to be prepared to face the challenge every time. I can honestly say that I got my fighting spirit from my mom. She is the most peaceful person I know. She exemplifies the biblical metaphor of: if someone slaps you on the left cheek, show the right cheek. That's the image I had of her growing up, and I could never understand why she was like that with people. With age, I came to not only understand her, but admire her for the life she has lived. She will forever be the ultimate survivor for me.

I was barely seventeen the day I left my family and my hometown to go live in a campus to start my university life. My parents sat me down for a last pep talk, and my dad was the first to start. After he warned me again about bad influences in friends, boys, early pregnancies, alcohol, etc., he proceeded in telling me about evil on this earth. He started telling me about people who were against him and who tried to destroy him, and now they will try to go after his children. He wanted me to be very careful and on alert at all times. It was a long speech that left me very confused, puzzled and a little lost. He insisted that I don't forget what he was saying. My mom interrupted to forbid him to tell me those things. Then she turned to me and said: "Yes, there are bad people out there. You are going to be on your own from now on. It is part of life. I don't want you to be afraid. I don't want you to ever be afraid of anything in life. God will always be on your side. So be confident, trust in yourself and your judgment, and God will take care of the rest. I am not worried about you going because you have never been one to be scared of anybody or anything. Don't ever lose that. I don't want fear to be the last thing you take with you when you are leaving this house. There are dangerous people out there, there is evil, but there is also good out there. My dream and hope for you is to be the best and become the best that God intended you to be. I have been telling you since you were little that you were born to achieve greatness. I told you that my personal dream for you is to see you become a great speaker and someone who gives speeches to a lot of people to help them in their lives. I don't know what it means or what it will be, but I have always seen you that way. You heard your dad tell you that he hopes to see you become a lawyer. All this must show you and convince you that you were destined to achieve great things. So whatever you will go through in life from now on, whatever you will encounter, don't lose sight of your purpose in life. Challenges will come and will go if you don't lose sight of what you have to achieve in life. If people attempt to harm you in any way, remember that all they can do is delay you or slow you, but they will never stop you. No one has control over your life but you. Don't ever forget that. Never walk or do anything in fear because it will only lead you to failure and defeat. You are stronger than you think. Nothing can beat you down but you; and that will be a terrible waste. So go and don't fear anything."

This is what I call a fighting spirit to carry you through anything in life. I have been repeating that motto all my life, and it still helps me today. We all have someone who says something to us at one point in our lives. You have to find it and use it to revive yourself every time you start feeling down. You have so much more that you can achieve, and you owe it to yourself to focus on that, draw your strength from that, and move forward.

Don't lose sight of where you need to go

What makes people stay in a bad relationship or a bad situation— is how they understand the difference between where they want to go and where they need to go. What we want is not always what is good for us. What we need is not always what we try to get. When you are in a bad predicament it is important to remember what you need. What we want is sometimes just wishful thinking. What we need is essential and a must-have.

Growing up, the children in my hometown were mean and resolute to keep using the little power they had over other children who didn't have the same skills as them. I happened to be one of the kids with no physical ability whatsoever at the time. I couldn't climb trees. I couldn't jump from the top of any edge. I couldn't march on a half wall even when someone was holding my hand. I was made fun of, teased and laughed at endlessly. This is something I couldn't change because no one was even allowing me to try and improve myself. It gave the other kids great pleasure to see me stay at my ridiculous level just to preserve me as their entertainment.

The worse nightmare was on the road to the river where we got our fresh water from. If we had to choose a name for that road, we could have called it: the road to nowhere, the road impossible to travel, the evil road, the road of the fallen, dead-end road, the road where no one makes it standing. All those names were the way I saw that road. Looking back, I am not sure if everyone would say the same thing. Maybe for some it was just a normal road, and for others it wasn't really that different than some other roads. Nevertheless, that's what it seemed to me at that time. Unfortunately that was the only way to fetch water. How many nights I went to bed asking myself why the earth had to make my life that way. Of all the places where the river could have been flowing, it had to be at that spot, so the only way to get there would be through that road. The upstream of the river where the water was cleaner and fresher was strategically located down the road at the bottom of the monster hill with an inclination of between a hundred and a hundred and twenty degrees to my view. In summer when it is a dry season, going up that hill with a pail of water on your head was the work of Hercules. We had to do this every single day since it was the only way to get fresh and clean water. These kids who made it their living mission to turn our childhood into a nightmare to remember, made sure that when nature didn't send the rain our way, they would make the rain fall on the road. They had mastered the technique of climbing that hill, and made it look like the inclination was a simple hundred and eighty. When it came time for us little people like me, we were all looking weak, lazy, and really dumb.

Every day they would make sure that they went to the river first, fetched water, and walked all the way up to the top of the hill. Once up there, they would deliberately drop water on the side that is used to walk, then start sliding on it to make it as wet and slippery as they could. Then came the rest of us, in a hurry to get water, just to find ourselves falling over and over again and losing all the water we were trying to take home. This would subject us to repeat the effort over and over again until we could make it through to the top of the hill. The excruciating part of the whole thing was that every day was the same routine again and again. You can imagine the struggle and the pain anyone would have to endure just to bring one single pail full with water home. Now try to imagine what it was like when you had to make more than one trip there. In my case, it was even worse. My parents had a poultry farm at that time, and our routine chores involved filling up at least two barrels of water every day in order to have enough water for the house and the hundreds of chickens.

However hard and challenging it was during the dry season, you would have to multiply the level of complication by ten to come close to what the same exercise or chore would be in the rainy season. You would think that with the rain it would be easier because the hill would be washed off. It was actually worse. Nature was doing the water spilling on the ground for these rascals, dropping more water on the ground than they could have done, and now the water could sit there with the result of it producing slippery mud. Everybody now had to be careful going up the hill. The best way up was to grab anything standing on the sidewalk (namely plants or branches) to move without falling, or use a cane. It wasn't a difficult technique to master when you are a natural walker or you are an adult. The only problem was that, by the time some of us got to the same plant, it would have been pulled so many times that it had become fragile. Sometimes the vicious kids would really make sure that they pulled everything around it that could be used as support to climb up. They pulled them just enough to loosen them up and leave them there. So when we came, we saw the branches or the plants, and the natural instinct was to try to grab them, hang on to them, and surprise!! They would give up and we would slide back down the hill. It was the most heartbreaking and pathetic spectacle you could ever witness. Unfortunately it was a mandatory way to the clean and fresh water. You need water? You will have to go through that pain. You need more water? You will have to endure the cruelty again and again.

The whole thing was hopeless, but you had to still go through it. The condition would bring up every emotion possible of helplessness, humiliation and a sense of unworthiness that can strip any feeling of dignity, pride and self-respect. I didn't even have a choice or different options. This was something I had to do. This wasn't something you can go negotiate so the parents can send somebody else to fetch the water. It's your job, it's your chore, it's everyone's chore. No matter what goes on over there, it wasn't even thinkable that you would come back home with an empty pail, or you would come back to complain to your parents that you could not bring the water because the road was slippery. You would look foolish because everyone knows it's the dry season. You can't possibly dare to say the other kids spill water all over the road and made it slippery. They are just kids like you; so if they manage to go on all the way to the top of that same hill, why can't you? So either way you are doomed. Suck it up and bring back water. Do whatever you have to do. The only end to that story is that you bring back the water and enough water to fill up the barrel, or enough water needed. What are you going to do?

This is one of those situations where the end becomes the means. You don't have any other alternative but to make it through. If you want the water, you will have to make it through the hill and bring the water home, then go back there if you have to bring more water home to fill up the barrel. There is no other way. You can't sit there without water because some bad kids made your pathway less practical. You can't come home to complain to your parents that other kids are getting the water. You are therefore cornered and sentenced to make it through.

I am not a neuroscientist, but I firmly believe that our brain or mind has this ability to find a solution whenever we feel cornered. We start to think about a way out, how we can survive the impasse. We think about other options we might have overlooked. The solution we didn't envision.

When you know you have to make it through, you convince yourself you have to make it through; then you will surely make it through.

My way wasn't to start competing with them or to show them that I can beat them. It would have been a lost cause and a huge waste of time. I didn't have all day as the day wasn't about fetching water. We still had to go to school and live a normal life with the rest of the chores. So if I make it my goal to show them that I can defy them, confront them or climb like them, then I will just get involved in their silly game and lose track of what I am there for. I will spend too much time on them instead of finding ways to achieve my goal of bringing water home. Their antics are cruel and a distraction to what I have to do. My goal can't become about showing them that they don't intimidate me, or scare me, or that I can be better than them. Again it will be a waste of time and take me away from making it through so I can get the water home, since the rest of the day depends on that water. People have to use that water, the chickens depend on that water, and getting water is just one of the chores or tasks of the day. I can't be late, I can't be distracted, I can't miss the rest of the day.

When I stayed focused on my goal of making it through so I could bring water home, then the only question in my mind was: how do I bring this water safely home? Among the many different ways, I figured that I had to find the best way to avoid going to that road when these rascals are also there or after they have been there. Then I realized that if I go earlier than them, I would have enough time to get as much water as possible before they mess up the walking area. That's what I started doing even if it meant going to fetch water at night, or losing one hour of sleep because I had to go earlier than anyone. This started working. Since it would require many trips to the river to fill the barrels we had, by the time they would start coming to the river, I would be so far ahead that even if I start falling it would be less troubling. From that first strategy, I started adding different little ways to get my water, fill up the barrels and go on with my day. Before you knew it the season was over and we kept on moving forward that way.

This just illustrates how important it is to stick to whatever you have to do. The mind will find a way to help you come up with good and relevant options or strategies to go through any complication or barrier you are facing. If I had focused more on the rascals and what they were doing to me, then my whole life would have shifted to the drama, mainly to fight with them, trying to prove myself to them, thus making them my goal. It should never be about anything else but your own life and where you want to take it.

CHAPTER 4

Don't get stuck in the "why me?" But rather focus on the "how do I get out?"

THERE IS A SIMPLE REASON WHY I CALL THE "WHY ME" QUESTION: the gate and the route to madness. Whenever the situation is a good one, the answer to that same question is direct, easy and clear. When you win a contest, you generally know why you won. When you get chosen for a bonus at work, you know why you were chosen. When you get asked in marriage, you know why. But when we face a negative outcome, the "why me" never takes us to a straight answer. Instead, it leads to another "why me" and another "why me," creating endless questioning that often never finds an answer. Nobody deserves to go through hardship, pain, or any type of cruelty. But unfortunately we do find ourselves from time to time facing the most horrific situations in life, whether by our imagination or for real.

When you are in it, you are in it, and the best question you should ask yourself in that moment should always be: "How do I get myself out of here?"

Spending time asking why me is the biggest waste of time and the most costly moment you will go through. Picture this, when you are in a painful situation, being abused, victimized or whatever you are experiencing, all you are is a victim. But the minute you can identify what happened to you or that you have been a victim of something, you have to understand that the ordeal is already in your past. It is no longer the situation or the moment, but the minute after, the morning after, the week after. You have survived, you are still alive, and you are breathing. That's all the motivation you will ever need to bounce back, start rebuilding your life and reclaiming your power. The rest is in you and around you.

I have seen this manifest over and over again with terminally ill patients. Imagine sitting in that doctor's office and they deliver the news of the diagnosis, and it is any one of those incurable illnesses out there, and they go on to give you a countdown for your life. We have all watched or heard the stories of people who went through these moments. The most beautiful things I have ever heard came from them. Sentences like, "I'll be damned if this thing beats me"; "I want to enjoy every second and every minute of the life I have"; "This thing is not going to control my life...."

I believe it's just human nature that when we are victim of any injustice or any crisis, we want pity, we want sorrow or for someone to feel bad for us, to feel sorry for us. There is no denying that the perpetrator took something from you, but it's not your life, so don't give them your will and don't surrender your life to them. Your life is not defined by that incident.

Here I was, about to be a single mother, something I didn't even dream of happening just a few weeks or few days before. Here I was, just planning my maternity leave and looking forward to enjoying this time before I go back to work nine months later. But now the situation I was in meant I didn't know what I was going to do with my life. On top of all that, my bank account was empty, my self-esteem had taken a beating, and my reputation was down the tube. How can I go anywhere from here?

I had to dig deeper to remind myself that whenever I have been in an impossible situation, I had to draw some strength and inspiration from within me or around me. This time is no different, and this too will pass.

We often forget to remember the joy of being alive

I grew up in a big family of eleven children. But we were constantly more than fifteen children because my mom fostered other kids every year. Of course it always looked like whatever food we had was not enough because it had to be broken down into so many little pieces to feed everybody. Until I became a teenager, I had to share a bed with at least one sibling or one of the foster children. What kid wouldn't hate it? Every child always wishes to be the only child and not have to share their parent's attention. We were living in a small town with a population of less than fifty thousand. I never went anywhere on a trip until I was a teenager.

The summertime was good and bad. It was exciting to see all the cousins who lived in the city, who came back home for the summer vacation. It was a great opportunity to see the latest fashions, to learn the city language, and to find out some new dance moves. But it was also very bad, because we always felt inferior to them. Living in the city is where the light is, and in this case, it was actually true. Modern electricity only came to our town when I was fourteen years old. So until that time, I never knew what a light bulb looked like, let alone electrical light. It also meant that when the kids from the city were talking about cold drinks, I didn't know what they were referring to since I had never seen a fridge. I had to listen to the city kids go on and on about how good their lives were, and this was an annual beating for my self-esteem. Why should I be the one living this miserable town life? I never went anywhere. I lived with chickens, darkness, and horrible kids who didn't even realize that we were all doomed in this hole we called a town. I was angry, bitter and judgmental. My anger was directed at my parents most of the time. I was blaming them for making me stay in that town, for letting me be born in this miserable place where I would forever live in the dark. My knowledge was limited because I couldn't see what other people in the city saw. I felt so miserable, so poor, so dumb and so useless.

My parents decided one time to finally take me on a trip to the city. They said we would go visit my big sister who lived in the biggest city, and I could see her at work. We took the coach instead of the train, and my mom managed to keep me awake during the whole trip so I could see everything en route to the big city since it was my first time out of town. I was convinced that we were the most primitive people in the whole country. I expected everything else to be bigger, grander and more beautiful than everything from my town. The first thing I saw was the bush... a lot of bushes. There were little isolated houses here and there on the way, but they looked like cabanas, with people sitting outside as if they lived there. My only thought was: how in the world can someone live there? Thirty or forty-five minutes later, we saw children playing outside another place. They didn't have shoes on. I was horrified for them. I asked my mom why they took such a risk of playing without shoes as they could seriously hurt their toes. My mom just smiled and said, "Some kids have shoes, and some others don't. But it shouldn't stop them from being kids and doing what kids are supposed to do: play and have fun."

We eventually entered the big city, and I could feel the excitement, a lot of noise, a lot of people and cars. As soon as we got off the big coach, we had to walk to the other side of the street to get a cab, and then I saw the most shocking thing: a man walking half naked, talking to himself, sometimes gesturing or dancing. This was attracting people, some were laughing and others asked him to go home. The guy was demented. A few feet away from that madness, I got startled by a woman sitting on the bare floor with two little kids around her and a third one on her lap. She was stretching to grab my mom's attention. I got so startled that I screamed. She had no fingers or toes. I was holding my mom so tight that I almost made her trip on the floor, and she calmly explained to me that it's called leprosy, a debilitating disease that makes people lose their fingers and toes, among other things.

Clearly, it wasn't the city I expected to see. Then we stopped by an aunt's house to say hello. It had three rooms, plus the kitchen. Eight people were living there at the same time. These houses were packed one to another, with too much noise and dirt everywhere. "Who lives like this, anyway?" I asked. My mom quickly responded: "People in the city, obviously". I noted that the cousins who usually come back to my town in the summer to tell us about the great life they have—they didn't even have a front yard to play in. They always came back home for summer vacations talking about this paradise with all the stuff they do here and all the fun that it was. How can it be great when some people are sleeping on the floor? My mom just looked at me with that vindicated kind of smile and said: "Well my dear, this is the city life you were crying over the other day, remember? This is reality. I am sorry if you were expecting something more glamorous or special. But this is what life looks like for some people, even those we admire. Just learn to enjoy and be grateful for what you have. It is more important to learn to accept and be who you are, and see that your home is not that bad, and your life back home is not as horrible as you thought."

She promised that I would feel differently when we go to see my big sister, and see what she does; it will give me a different perspective of things. My sister was a physiotherapist in a rehabilitation centre, helping children with disabilities. Some of the children had twisted legs and arms, the others had multiple limbs and couldn't walk properly. Others had no limbs, but they could still move. At that age I had never seen things like that. I remember to this day how I kept on thinking that this trip was turning out to be torture, a big punishment for envying the city kids. I must have hurt my parents' feelings for them to bring me on this horror trip, and I got startled so much that I was holding onto my mom's arm so tightly that I almost ripped her dress.

She took me to the training room where my sister was, and it was there that I noticed right away that something else was happening. A totally different dynamic was going on in this part of the centre. All of the disabled children were busy trying to run, or just standing still. Some others were practicing how to put one foot in front of the other. These are simple gestures we make every minute of every day in our lives, which were so challenging to them. Those little movements that we take for granted because we perform them naturally. We don't realize how much it requires our body and brain to activate them in order to achieve these simple gestures.

We found my sister right outside where the rest of the children were playing a little game of pass the ball. They all had in common the handicap of not being able to walk naturally, so they had to try to move by any means possible to catch and push the ball to one another. Standing there, regardless of your age, you can't help but be completely blown away by the will of these children to at least try. They were all laughing and giggling, and everyone was so focused to touch that ball at least once. The joy on their faces and the fun they had in trying was an image that has stayed in my memory all my life. You could see the excruciating effort and the painful manoeuvring they had to go through in order to touch that ball or to push it enough to direct it to someone else to keep the ball circulating. Most of them could never touch the ball, but the enthusiasm with which they tried made them victorious in their own eyes. In their attempt to reach that ball and push it, they were a hundred percent committed to the game with all their hearts and minds. The whole process was stirring up a level of enthusiasm in them regardless of whether they actually touched that ball or not. I am sure that every time someone else pushed it, they felt as if they were the one pushing it themselves.

What a lesson in resilience, perseverance, belief and the power of hope. The fun that they were having in participating and trying was a bigger lesson, and we were all cheering for them from the side. I couldn't resist being pulled into the enthusiasm. At the end, a lot of them managed to lift their bodies, limbs and heads in a way they never thought possible before, thus getting hope for a brighter future. I brought that image back with me. From that time on, no tree was high enough for me. I could climb them all. I started playing sport. That is the single event that killed the fear of failure in my heart forever. Every time in my life that I go through difficulties, whether big or more manageable, the only thought that usually keeps me from falling apart is remembering those kids. I have been sharing this story for many years now, trying to cheer people up around me who get depressed or lose their material things. I always said that as long as you have all your limbs, you are breathing, you can walk and think—be hopeful that tomorrow could be a better day if you want it to be. Try to focus on making sure that your future will turn out better than your past or your present. The future starts tomorrow. That's all that matters from now on.

The art of counting our blessings every time

We have all heard the old saying of: "You don't know what you've got until it's gone". This old saying illustrates just how much we take things for granted. We are ungrateful to nature or our creator for what we have. Why does it take us until we see people less fortunate than we are before we appreciate what we have?

It's a shame that people have to be reminded of a simple thing like saying hello. You don't know how important it is to receive a "hello" until you find yourself alone with nobody around you for a while. I know how difficult it is to understand how precious everything we have in life really is. So we have to be grateful when we have it. Think of how you feel with a simple common cold. Your nose is stuffed and it is hard to breathe, your throat hurts and it is hard to swallow any food, your stomach is upset and it is hard to eat anything, and your muscles ache so much that you don't want to leave your bed.

The best story I have heard on counting our blessings came from watching one of my favourite shows on television—the Hour of Power with Dr. Robert H. Schuller—from my hospital bed one day. In his preaching, Dr. Schuller told the story of two patients that we will call Jake and Doug, who ended up in the same hospital room. Jake had a chronic illness that required him to be lying down on his bed, and he couldn't move. There was a curtain around his bed, and he could not see anything else in the room beside the machines, the wall, the tubes, and another wall. He had to rely on his roommate, Doug, to find out what was going on outside. Doug could sit and walk around the room. So every morning while lying down on his bed, Jake asked Doug what he was doing. Doug would say that he was sitting on his bed just contemplating the beauty of nature. Then Jake asked him to please describe everything he saw, and to please be his eyes and let him know what goes on outside. So Doug would proceed by telling him, "The sky is beautiful today. There is this mix of clouds with heavenly shapes that reminds me of a peaceful garden. Right now I can't keep my eyes off these magnificent swallows that are jumping from one branch of this welcoming oak tree. They are three, and seem to play with each other. One has these beautiful dots that look grey, but are actually a rare dark brown that mixes well with the white feathers. The second is grey with the colour fading lighter under the wings. The third one is all brown with a little bit of a line right between the eyes. I wish you can see them. What a beauty! The colours are so magnificent. Yes, I see two people who are walking toward a bench right now holding hands. They look so in love and peaceful. They are laughing. Now they are gazing at each other with so much passion in their eyes."

Doug would continue the description of each thing in such heavenly beauty and magnificence. Jake would sigh in relief, and say thank you, "It is so exciting and colourful and beautiful. I feel good just listening to you. You describe it so well that I don't even feel that I can't see all that you see. The next morning, Jake was eager to get a new report of the day. So Doug started again: "The sky is still blue with few clouds that bring a sense of fall. The birds are back here, but this time, wait a minute... who do I see with them? My goodness, look at this cutie. It's another swallow that followed them. I guess it couldn't resist the attraction. Now here comes the lover, but he is alone today."

Jake said, "Oh oh! What do you think happened with the woman?"

Then Doug replied, "Maybe she is just late. He is waiting, that means he has hope she will come."

"Please tell me when she gets there," asked Jake. "I don't want to miss anything."

This became their daily routine as each day Doug described what he saw, such as: "The most beautiful sunset you could imagine". He gave Jake every single detail of the people who walked by, what they were wearing, what they were doing and their mood. Some days the people were arguing, some days they were laughing, and some other days they were silent. He would describe the particularity of their clothes, talk about the birds he saw, the dogs, the cars. Story after story, Doug was helping Jake go through his stay at the hospital as if it was the best vacation; and it made him forget he was in a hospital.

Then one day Doug died. Jake could no longer discover the comings and goings of the people around the hospital. He felt like he was missing out on all the actions because no one was there anymore to describe what's going on. He was getting depressed, so one morning he waited for the nurse to come in, and he asked, "Could you please do me a favour?" Could you stand by the window there and tell me what you see, and please don't leave any detail out. Usually at this time of the day, the birds should be there by now, and the sky. What colour is it today? And who is walking down there?"

The nurse was puzzled and said, "I don't know what you are talking about. All there is outside this window is a wall from the next building."

"That is impossible," replied Jake. "Look closely, there should be a tree, the tree with beautiful leaves where the birds come every day. You should be able to see the sky. At least tell me about the sky". The nurse repeated that there was nothing there but the wall from the other building, and it was impossible to see the sky.

"How come my roommate could see all those things and not you?" asked Jake, a little irritated. When the nurse answered that there is just no way Doug could have seen anything, Jake insisted that every day Doug was sitting there on his bed, and right after 10 a.m., he started describing what's going on outside: the tree, the birds, the people, the sky and the noise.

The nurse said: "There is no way he could have seen all that, no matter how closely he was sitting to the window. Doug was blind from birth. So whatever he was telling you was probably just the beautiful world he had built for himself, and he made you live in it for the short time he was here. Maybe that's the world he wanted to see if only he could."

Going from Homeless to CEO

How amazing it would be to see the world like Doug, and live it accordingly. Wouldn't it be great if we could all live like Doug in a make-believe world?

Most of the time we get so caught in the moment that we don't lift our head or our eyes to see that our situation is not really the worst thing. Yes it is bad, terrible, horrible. But it's not the worst that can happen to someone. We tend to focus more on what we don't have, what we are losing or missing; and we don't see what we have.

How great it is to be grateful every morning when we wake up, and count that as a blessing. Imagine just how many people didn't make it through the night because they died in their sleep or got into an accident in the middle of the night. How great would it be for us to be grateful for having both our legs and being able to walk? Imagine just how many people don't have that luxury. Every time we are eating something, imagine how many people will go to bed hungry, and not know if the next day will be any different. We need to learn to appreciate what we have, when we have it.

When you count and identify what is good in your life, in any given time, I can guarantee that the good always outweighs the bad. But we don't see it because we focus more on the one thing in our life that is going wrong.

The bad for me was that I lost my home, my bank account was empty, my boyfriend turned out to be a liar and a cheater, and I was miserable, hurt, in pain, and homeless. The good was that I found a quiet shelter so I still had a roof over my head compared to being on the street. I didn't have to pay the rent, I could breast-feed my child, and my maternity leave allowance would kick in at one point after twelve weeks. The shelter gave me used clothes, and people donated diapers and a lot of other stuff, so I would be fine for a while. I was rid of the bad boyfriend, and I had a healthy baby who was adorable and beautiful. I also had a peaceful environment inside of me so I could prepare for a brighter future, and I was healthy. The list can go on.

Nothing clears the mind better than listing the good things we have going in our lives at the time. Whenever you feel down or depressed, the best remedy is to really take a minute and look at what you have. It is not about living in Doug's make-believe world. It's not about living an imaginary life. It's about the balance between what we can control and what we cannot control. It is about the balance between the power to influence the outcome and the power to change the situation. It is very difficult to think of anything good when a sheriff is coming to evict you, or when the repo company is coming to take your car away, or when you have been told you have a bounced cheque, or when you don't know what you could eat by the end of the day, or even when you have just been told that you have a terminal illness. The minute I got the final answer that I will be losing my house, there was nothing I could do with that decision. I couldn't control that portion anymore. Therefore, there is no reason to beat myself up over that decision. I can't change it, I can't control anything about it anymore, and I have no power there. Indeed I couldn't change the situation, but I could definitely influence the outcome and choose the way I reacted to the whole thing. This allowed me to clear the barriers I was facing, and I was able to go on with my life.

Our responsibility toward ourselves is to take care of what we can control when we face a situation. One minute before the present moment is already the past. There is nothing we can naturally or logically do about it. The only thing that we can do something about is the next minute, the moment after, the morning after, the day after, the week after, the month after, the year after. We can't change the circumstances we find ourselves in, but we can do something about the way we react or respond to them. That reaction is completely our choice, our decision which is controlled by us. This is where we can do something to help ourselves. We need to help ourselves because we have the rest of our life to live and we owe it to ourselves to make that be the best we could ever dream to have. Why? Because the other option is just something I can't even get into, and everyone should refuse to consider it.

CHAPTER 5

Forgiveness is a decision not a process

A S WE KNOW BY NOW, FORGIVENESS IS MORE ABOUT YOURSELF than it is about the other person who hurt you. It is about allowing yourself to move forward, to cleanse your soul and your heart from any negative thoughts that might still tie you to the past when you actually need to be in the present, looking toward the future. It is also about getting rid of regrets that keep people always looking backward. It's simply about you, your life, yourself, and the decision to let bygones be bygones.

It might sound simplistic to say: just decide to forgive and everything will be alright. But guess what? It is really that simple. Somebody hurt you and did something terrible to you. What options do you have? Hate that person for the rest of your life? Okay, go ahead and hate the person as much as you want. But how much bad can this really do to that person? On the other hand, how much good can it really do you for hating that person for as long as you live? Does this really repay you for the pain you have endured? Does this compensate anything you have lost? The answer is NO. This kind of silliness is what we usually engage in without really taking a minute to realize the harm we cause to ourselves with that attitude. Unfortunately, the only person we harm is ourselves with this campaign of no forgiveness. This is not rocket science. It's basic logic.

I am not saying this because I am an angel with a pure heart, but because I went through it and realized that the ten years of my life I wasted waiting for an epiphany to break the anger and the resentment, never happened. The day I decided that the whole thing was not even worth one minute of my thought, is the day I let go, and it was the day I started actually living again. Since then I learned that it has more to do with a decision than a cure. Learning to forgive is about learning to control or get rid of the anger. We usually can't forgive because we don't want to get rid of the anger. Then the question is not about why we can't forgive, but rather why we want to hold on to the anger. In many cases, it is easier to hold on to the anger than to embrace the freedom to be us again and move on with our life. It is easier to focus on how bad life or people have been to us than what we are doing with our life. It makes others bear the responsibility, not us. Life is always easier when someone else is responsible, not us. Therefore forgiving is about making us responsible for something one way or another, whether we like it or not. The moment has to come when we make that choice, and that moment has to be sooner rather than later. It doesn't really take an epiphany or an intervention, or even ten years. All it takes is you deciding that you want to make your thoughts and feelings about you. People say it takes time, and that you have to process the hurt, the anger and the humiliation before you can be in a place to forgive. I completely disagree. How can it be a process if you can't touch it, you can't manipulate it, and you can't misplace or exchange it? It is a feeling which, in this case, is your feeling. You are the only one who feels it or lives it. Therefore only you can have the power over it. That means it will take a decision from you to refuse to have it again. In reality though, the feeling is really just anger over the pain, the humiliation, and the loss or the lack of something we felt through the ordeal. The sooner you acknowledge that, the sooner you can make the decision that it is not worth you spending much time, energy and thought on it. Just move on with the rest of your life. Since it is a feeling, then it comes from your thoughts. So if you change your thoughts, your feelings will also change.

Choose to let go of the anger

Anger is a very destructive feeling. It is an expression of something we feel inside, whether it is an annoyance, an irritation, hurt, or just nervousness. We have to get it out or the consequences can be devastating. The only question is: How long should we entertain that thought, and when should we get it out? We all wish to be able to always express our anger the minute we feel it so we can get it out of ourselves and move on to something else. Now, we know that some of us are good at controlling our temper, thus keeping our anger in check. But unfortunately some other people don't know how to let go and forget about the whole incident. Depending on the nature of the hurt and how deep we get hurt, it can be really challenging to let go of the anger we feel. Why? Because of the humiliation, the embarrassment or the ridicule we felt when the incident happened. This can make it hard to get past the hurt and the anger, or to forget about the whole thing and move on. In any case, it is important to be reminded of the consequences of being angry in the first place, which can be devastating at times. That need for revenge that sometimes people feel—we all know that it doesn't really heal anything, nor does it solve anything. But that's not the destructive part of anger I am referring to, but instead the consequences to yourself that we are not aware of sometimes. When we are hurting or suffering, we want to get better and we want to heal. You get a cut, you want to treat it, heal it so that part of your body can go back to normal. We get emotionally bruised, and we have to heal as well. Anger is just the manifestation of that hurt, the pain we feel, the bruising of our emotions. We need to heal. Only here it is different because we can't see or touch the cut. Everything is in our head or heart. Everything is inside of us. This is why it has to go first if we ever want to go back to a normal life and be ourselves again.

You need to let go of the anger first because you want to gain the freedom to be you again. You need to focus your energy and thoughts on moving toward your destination, your goals, and building your life the way you've envisioned it.

You have to let go of the anger because that feeling affects you and nobody else. You are the only person on earth who is even aware of it. It is living inside of you. The old saying of "what you don't know can't kill you," applies here. What the other person you are angry at doesn't know will not affect them. You have to understand that when you are staying up all night, using all your time to hate, curse or wish bad things to the other person, depriving yourself of a restful night of sleep—the only person affected by all this is you. Even when you tell people about it, it doesn't make them appreciate exactly how you feel in reality, does it? People usually tend to think that the other person is having the same thoughts or thinking of you while you are cursing them or hating them in your head or heart. They aren't.

I had a good friend who was always ready to jump at anybody for little things. He was yelling at people everywhere. While driving he will blow the car's horn to anybody who gets by him on the road. He had to take his car to a mechanic almost every other month to get his horn replaced. While he obsessed over that other driver, he was forgetting that he was on a highway and there are other cars. He will miss the exits so many times because he was chasing after other cars blowing his horn to teach them a lesson. The problem was, nobody outside his car could even hear his screaming inside his car, and the slaps and punches he inflicted to his car to the point of hurting and bruising his hand— nobody else got them but him. He was the one who ended up spending money to get the car's horn fixed all the time. He would go hustling cars and driving dangerously, which put other people's lives in danger and exposed him to traffic violations, which used to cost him a lot of money. He missed his exit, which means more gas than he needed to use, and he ultimately spent more time being exposed to more potential bad drivers. All that for what? Just because he was angry at the other driver who never knew he was?

This is an example, an extreme one I admit, but it goes to the core of the point I am making on how useless it is to stay angry and try to act out of anger. It illustrates how much we harm ourselves, our lives and our goals by giving too much space or attention to our angry feelings. If we don't let go of it, it consumes us and opens us to more potential harm, and our priorities get shifted in the process.

The first step to our freedom, healing and rebuilding is to get rid of the anger and take care of ourselves. This is a choice we have to make.

Remember that your life is not over

I will never forget Monica as long as I live. I met her at the shelter where I was staying. She had been living inside shelters for five years, and she was the only exception to the rule that every woman was subjected to: the maximum time you are allowed to stay is six months. Monica was a petite woman, very feminine and sophisticated in her mid forties. She liked to dress nicely and she would always talk respectfully to everyone. She had the brightest smile of the whole house, and was always exhibiting joy and happiness any given time of the day. When two women got into a nasty spat, she was the first one to try to talk them out of it, and reminded everybody how much life is precious and that we have to strive to live it peacefully rather than waste even a minute arguing over nothing. She encouraged women all the time to try to get to know one another instead of yelling at each other. She kept repeating to everyone that we usually take life for granted, we take friendship for granted, and we generally take people for granted. It doesn't matter who is right or who is wrong as most of the time everybody is probably right, so the argument is irrelevant, silly, and a big waste of time. We are all stuck here, and like it or not the same person you are insulting or cursing is probably the best thing you have in a friend right at that moment. She is the closest thing you have to a person who truly understands what you are going through right now. So instead of alienating her or berating her, just talk to each other so we can all have a quiet evening.

My first reaction listening to her was: is she real or fake? Then I thought that she probably lost her mind and the only way the world makes sense to her is through beauty. I was told before that some demented people can lose touch with reality and just start seeing things we don't see. So I imagine her seeing beautiful flowers everywhere, or seeing peace everywhere, and that's why she talked the way she did.

She was always nice to me and was always offering to watch my baby for me if I needed her to, and always enjoyed playing with her. I was also pleased that she asked, and I was very glad to let her play with my baby because she was always clean, very well presented, and smelled good.

There was a code of conduct with all women: you don't ask why a woman is there, you just talk about anything else. If she volunteers her story, then you can know what happened to her.

More than thirty women living at the house were there because they went through horrific circumstances. They ended up homeless. Some had four children there with them. Some had lost everything. We could all relate to that every day, and we could understand why they snap, they cry, they scream at other people. It is a struggle to go through life and get through the day when one day you had this perfect life with plans, hopes and dreams— then one morning your life is gone and you have to start grasping to make sense of all that, or who you are. You have to fight to rebuild. Sometimes they don't know where to begin or if they will ever make it again. While I was there, one woman just couldn't take the pressure anymore and had a heart attack. The whole thing was just too much.

I went on and on setting my point to Monica, describing how life is horrible for everybody around and that's why they are showing it by complaining, yelling and struggling. In the meantime, she seemed to be the only calm one, the only one who even took the time to dress, to style herself and to always present the best image of herself. She was singing all the time when everyone else was sad and sitting quietly in the corner, or crying. I said, "You seem to be happy being here". I couldn't take it anymore. So I had to ask. Since we had developed this closeness with her helping with my baby a lot, I felt that I could dare to ask.

"Monica," I said, "excuse me, but I have to ask. What's the deal with you? Are you some sort of police informant who infiltrates shelters? I don't get you." She said that to her, happiness is what you make of it. You can choose to be happy or sad; it is really your decision, not the circumstances. I said, "Come on now, you are patronizing me. You are not here like the rest of us?" She added that life is really what you make of it. Each morning when you wake up, you choose to be happy or not, you choose to be grateful for the day you have, or not. The day really goes as you choose.

So I asked again what her deal was, because I guess she didn't have the same issues as the rest of us. Then she invited me to sit down before she started. She told me that she was there under police protection. I quickly said, "I knew it, you work for the police." She repeated, "I am under police protection, not undercover," then continued with this unbelievable tale.

"All of you are here for some horrific situations you went through," she began. "I really feel for all of you and sympathise with your tragedies. Nobody deserves that treatment. You lost a lot, or maybe everything, you even got rid of the boyfriend or partner. Lucky you! I am stuck with mine. I will be stuck with mine for the rest of my life, or until one us dies first. The way it is right now, I am probably going to spend the rest of my life going from shelter to shelter, and I have been living like this for the past five years. The only three times I was away from a shelter was when I was in hospital.

"I was living with a boyfriend who used to abuse me so much that the day I told him that I wanted out of the relationship, he beat me up and raped me so badly that he left me in a house for dead. Luckily someone found me and I was taken to the hospital. I was there for a month. When I got out, I was placed in a shelter like this one, but in a different city and different province. He found out that I was alive and followed me there. One day he ambushed me outside on the street. He beat me up and slit my throat with a big knife." She showed me this huge scar on her nape that sent chills all over my body.

"I was moved from there after another stay at the hospital, and placed in a different shelter. Once the police found out that he knew where I was staying, they had to move me to a different location. The guy has decided to make it his life mission to see me dead before he will let me go and have a life with anyone else or without him. In his mind, he owns me. He has been tracking me throughout Canada, and I almost have nowhere to hide, nowhere to settle, nowhere to build a life. So you see, he can be anywhere. Every day can be my last. The police and I are convinced that next time he will probably use a weapon to gun me down."

She showed me the multiple scars all over her arms, legs, stomach and back. Some were stab wounds, some were cuts from different objects used on her, and some others were burns. I interrupted her by asking why the police had not caught the guy. She said that he plays hide and seek with them, and they caught him before but because of a little technical issue, the judge had to free him again.

"This gave him even more determination to come after me," she stated. "That's why the police decided to focus more on protecting me than going after him. And with this beautiful smile of hers, she added with a laugh, "So you see my dear, you women here think you have problems. Try to top mine!" She turned back to my baby and continued singing and playing with her. I sat there for an entire hour, numb on my chair.

Then she paused her little interaction with my daughter, turned to me and added: "You see, when people always say they live every day to the fullest, as if it was their last... for me it is not a saying. That's my reality. Every single day that I wake up can be my very last day on this earth. So I say to myself every morning, if this is the day that has been made for me to go, I want to go happy, pretty, looking my best, smiling to people and with joy around me. So I dress myself every morning, I style my hair, I put on my makeup, I pray, and I am ready for the day. At the end of the day, I celebrate being alive and well. I am grateful for everything I see around me. That's the life I choose to live. Now if you want to see another option for me to go through my days, be my guest, try to imagine me living another way if you want, but I don't even want to think about any other way."

If that story doesn't profoundly touch you, then nothing else can move you. She made me want to have a better and more fulfilling life for the rest of my life. I knew right then and there that I had to stop beating myself up. I had to just be grateful to be alive, grateful that I was healthy. The past is the past. I just had to focus on my tomorrows. I have so much to live for and look forward to.

Get involved again or help others

The difficulty to forgive comes from the bruise our self-esteem or confidence gets when we go through pain or suffering inflicted by someone we hold dear to our heart. The struggle is usually to go back to feeling confident again, believe in our self-worth again, and find ourselves relevant again. Nothing cures a broken heart better than giving back to other people in need, or the less fortunate. This gives you the opportunity to forget about your own issues for a second. On top of giving, you get a sense of self-worth. It helps put things in perspective as you experience looking at life from someone else's situation. There are so many ways to give back to others: from reading to children, to helping out in soup kitchens, to volunteering in organizations. You have to find the cause that is dear to you, fulfilling to you; the one that gives you that sense of pleasure to help.

I have always believed that you can never know how much you have until you share it with others. You can also never appreciate what you have until you share it with others. And you can never understand the value of what you have until you see someone else use it. Nobody confirms this fact better than children. The best way to get them interested in a toy they are neglecting is to give it to another child. Once they see someone else with what is supposed to be theirs, then they remember the value of it and want to get it back.

We are usually quick to forget how beautiful we are, how talented we are, how smart we are, and how strong we are. We easily transfer our self-worth to what others will say we are, and we only see ourselves through the lenses of others. We expect others to validate who we are.

If the pain we went through is keeping us from remembering how valuable we are, and we stay prisoner of that hurt, then we have to draw from the outside to go back to ourselves. Participating in someone else's effort to live better, get better or improve their situation can be a powerful cure to our own impasse.

We can only forgive and forget when we go back to valuing ourselves.

CHAPTER 6

Solve one problem at a time and the courage to love life and yourself will come back to you

THE PROCESS OF GOAL SETTING CAN BE TRICKY AND PAINFUL IF you don't know precisely what you are after or what is it that you really want. We have all learned by now the multiple steps or techniques to set goals. The basic rule is to make your goals realistic and measurable. But what if you are still caught in your problems and you don't know where to start? Starting over can be very dreadful. It's like being laid off from a job. All of a sudden you have to start over by finding a new job. What do you do when the unexpected comes and just throws your life upside down; when nothing makes sense anymore?

On the other hand, many people wander through life without purpose, without direction, and without a clear idea of what exactly they want. In my experience, a lot of bitterness and grudges come from the fact that people don't know exactly what they want in life or how they should live their life after a painful experience. It becomes easier to stay obsessed with another person's life. The other person becomes responsible for your misery: "I can't move on because he did me wrong, he ruined me…." The status quo is not always a positive thing to have. You have to see life beyond the crisis. We owe it to ourselves to not let our lives be defined indefinitely by one incident or crisis, no matter how painful it was. That's the real victory over the crisis, and that's how we become triumphant.

Take charge of your life again

It can be very overwhelming to move away from a crisis, put the pieces together and rebuild your life. The courage to start over is not easy, but I have learned that if there is ever a moment to apply the "baby steps" formula, this is it. You have to take control of your destiny and your life again. It is always easy to have a big vision, and I sincerely believe that deep down everybody has a grandiose dream about their life—a big dream, a big ambition, a vision of a greater, successful life where everything is perfect. The problem is to know how to get there and where to start.

The baby steps, the little steps, means that you have to start somewhere and take one year at a time, or one month at a time, or one day at a time, one moment at a time, or even one task at a time.

Depending on the situation you are in, if you can, go for a one-year plan. You really need to sit down, take a piece of paper with a pen or pencil and write down what you want to achieve that year, what you want to accomplish. Look at every part of your life and set a yearly goal for that: work, finances, housing, health, love, friends, etc. Once you define that list, then you break it down into steps you have to take to make everything on your list take place. You can also write down the time it will require you to complete each task. Then you look for what you need to realize or execute the tasks. Once you have what you need, you start.

The idea behind this little exercise is to bring the focus back on you and what you need in your life. Giving yourself a plan for a year allows you to have things to look forward to, to set some parameters, some guidelines for your actions and thoughts, some boundaries within which you want to live and operate. This allows you to reshape your vision and channel your thoughts and feelings in achieving that vision. Nothing gives you a sense of purpose or direction and helps you take charge of your life more than that. As you start accomplishing the tasks, your focus will be more on what you have to do this day, this week, this month; what you have done today, last week, or last month; how you can change little things here and there to get even better results. You will learn a few things along the way that gives you other options in life and what the environment around you has to offer. You will realize that there is a lot more to explore out there, a lot more to look forward to than the trap you were locked in. You can soon find real meaning to your life that gives you hope and excitement, and you will discover the greater lengths you can go to and how much you have to offer and accomplish in life. You will have your new beginning.

I understand that some circumstances make it harder to think as far as a year ahead. This is okay. This is why I mentioned the "one at a time" formula, the real baby steps. I have to admit that this is the method I used more than anything at first. It simply consists of making a to-do list every evening before you go to bed, which lists all the things you want or have to do tomorrow. Every single thing you have to do. I put details like: shower, brush my teeth, style my hair, toast my bread, make a phone call to Jane for an appointment, call the library for the book I asked for, go pick up the laundry…. I found out how therapeutic it is to write down a list of what my whole day will be about. Then I go to bed motivated. This gives me something to look forward to for the next day, makes me feel busy, and occupies my mind with the things I have to do for myself. This method helps to get you back in the habit of waking up in the morning knowing that you have things to do, accomplish or achieve. It allows you to get on with the business of taking care of yourself each day, and it is very rewarding, exciting and encouraging to be checking off the things throughout the day that you have completed on the list. At the end of the day, you clear that list and make a new one for the next day. Things you couldn't accomplish, you will know why and what to do with them: either you have to add them to the next day's list, or to another day. Then you can start the next morning with a fresh list.

Bit by bit, you get into the habit of looking forward not backward; anticipating on tomorrow instead of dwelling on the past. This is a simple way to shift the focus, to reshape your thinking and move forward with your life, allowing you to take control over your life again. Make sure that your days are not dictated by the event in your past—even if the past is as close as last week—but rather by the things you plan to accomplish tomorrow. This way you make whatever hurt you or whatever caused you pain in the past to become irrelevant or just a distant memory. You will distance your feelings from that, and you will disconnect your thoughts from that and feel free to be you again.

Give yourself an inspiration

There is a reason why people look up to others. We have idols, we have role models, we have people who inspire us. When thriving to have a better life or to improve our situation, it helps sometimes to get inspired by others. It could be someone who went through the same thing and survived it. It could be someone who just achieved a lot, and we want to emulate that achievement. This is what I usually call arming ourselves with the healthy competitive mindset: If such and such did it, so can I. There is nothing wrong with thinking this way if you use the example to uplift yourself to break through an impasse or a dead-end. Some people are self-motivators, but for the rest of the crowd, a little push is always necessary. The point is not to take solace or pleasure in other people being more miserable than you are; nor to dwell in other people's problems. Whenever we find ourselves in a difficult situation, we need something to remind us that things are not really as bad as we think they are, and we shouldn't add too much drama to the situation. It is a total waste of time and energy. Time is precious, life is precious, our health is precious, and our body is precious.

What would we do if we were the Monicas of this world? Before I met Monica, I always had my mother as my ultimate inspiration. My mom was a lonely child and an orphan at the age of three having lost her own mother to an ovarian disease. Her dad was so overwhelmed with grief that he decided to give her away at the age of four to another family where she would grow to be a wife to one of the sons. So her grandmother, fearing for her safety, kidnapped her and hid her at a minister's home; and then she was bounced from one family to another until she was introduced to my dad. Unfortunately, when she got married, she was met with the fiercest rejection from her in-laws and all the other young women who had high hopes to be chosen by my father. She braved all that adversity and stayed strong, true to herself, and lived the most fulfilling life for someone with her past.

She has always said that she is richer than most people dream to be. I never understood why she said that until I went through pain, rejection and hardship myself. She told me that she asked God for one thing in life: that because she was an orphan, she wanted to have a life filled with people. God gave her thirteen children, and she fostered other children too. Her house was always filled with laughter, children playing outside, and a big community around her. My mother has been a true pillar of her community, and I have seen her give so much to others that to this day, thousands of people owe their education, success and happiness to my mother. In any given year, she always had at least twenty children depending on her. She fed them, clothed them, healed them and raised them all as if they were her own. She did that without ever holding a paying job and with my father getting a salary of less than sixty dollars per month.

My mother was creative, frugal, strong and fearless. She taught me how to count on the goodness of your heart when everything fails you. She taught me that when you focus on doing good, just trust your honesty and integrity, and the rest will work out just fine. She told me that in any horrible situation there is always a way out, and she firmly forbade me to ever focus on the bad situation, but rather on the way out of it. When you focus only on what is going badly in your life, you forget about the rest of your life that isn't bad. Other people are who they are, and it should never be a concern of yours. You have you to take care of yourself, so take care of you. She used to add that there is nothing you can ever do about heinous people with their cold hearts, mean ways, hurtful spirits and manipulative minds. As long as you don't lose sight of who you are and what you want in life, and you work hard to achieve the goals you have set for yourself, you will be just fine. Nature has a way of taking care of everybody in due time.

I have carried those lessons with me, and they have resonated in good and bad times, but have inspired me always with their wisdom and truth.

Define what kind of life you want

The simple secret is to define the vision of your life personally, professionally, and socially. In the same way that people usually tell what kind of job or career they want, you need to know what kind of life you want. It is difficult to succeed professionally if you don't even know what your career interests are; and the same rule applies to life in general.

People don't usually realize how costly and damaging it is to them to not know what they want in life. I personally think that the worst thing that happens to a lot of people in life is for them to go through life with no purpose. It is funny how when every time we have to move from one place to another unknown place, we usually have to give ourselves directions in order to know exactly how to get there. All explorers use a compass, all tourists walk around with maps. Strategists have to draw plans before suggesting policies. Every professional starts by defining a vision, the process and the resources needed, way before they start anything. The main question is: Why do most people imagine that they can really go through life without a plan? Without an idea of what it is they are looking for?

A plan has so many advantages. It gives you that sense of direction, it provides a focus, it centres your attention to what is important, it gives you a basis for evaluating your efforts, and it boosts your self-confidence. It also gives you essential boundaries to determine where you draw the line on what's acceptable and not acceptable.

I think that it should be a crime against humanity for anybody to enter a relationship with the intention to be passive-reactive. It doesn't actually matter which type of relationship it is, you must expect something to grow. You must nurture it, take care of it and feed it, and be vigilant that nothing harms its growth or development. The same rule applies to our life. If we give ourselves an idea of how we want life to be, grow and develop, then we will know what kind of boundaries we set to protect it, how we can nurture it, and what we won't accept.

We usually end up having a hard time bouncing back from problems because they catch us off guard. This doesn't mean we have to be prepared to face the problems that will come our way. Nobody can. But we can surely be prepared to bounce back and move forward with our life, and the only way we can do that is if we know exactly where we want to go.

When people commonly say that life is a journey, they are not mistaken. And if it is a journey, nobody should hit the road without a map, right? Let's imagine for a second that you start a journey with no idea of where you want to go, where you should start from, what transportation method you will use, how long the trip will last, how much it will cost you, what kind of clothes you will need on the way, and when you will get to your final destination. Not only will it be hard to start, but it can even be very dangerous to start. This puts you in a vulnerable position from the start of your trip: vulnerable to scams, to abuses, to accidents, etc. We can waste a lifetime wandering around without ever going anywhere. Anybody can fill in the blanks of this picture.

On the other hand, let's also imagine that you start a journey with a precise idea of where you want to go, where you should start from, what transportation method you will use, how long the trip will last, how much it will cost you, what kind of clothes you might need during the travel, and when you will get there. It gives you the confidence and assurance that you are ready for whatever happens along the way. Just like in any life, things sometimes happen on the journey. But in this case, if along the way there is an accident, a delay, a detour—you are better prepared to face all that because you stay focused on getting to your final destination. You will be active in moving heaven and earth to get to your final destination. This is the only thing that matters. You wouldn't sit there spending time asking why there is a storm, why the flight had to have a mechanical problem, why the road had to be closed or why the sky is not blue. Why not? Because you can see that all these questions are irrelevant in that moment. Getting to your final destination is your only priority.

So if you believe that life is a journey, treat your life as such...

unless you are one of those explorers a few centuries back who were going around in search of the unknown. But I bet that even they had an idea of which way they had to head first and the area they wanted to explore.

CHAPTER 7

Using faith to push forward

I HAVE MADE NO SECRET THAT I AM A FAITH-BASED PERSON. My faith is my moral, social, and even professional compass. I use the Bible for everything: it is my biggest motivational source, it is my inspirational source, and it is my instruction book for how to love, live and grow. Aside from that, it is a great historical book and a very entertaining read. I rooted my spiritual life in the Bible, and it is my sincerest belief that without faith and the love of God, I wouldn't be alive today. From the Bible, faith is defined as "being sure of what we hope for and certain of what we do not see" (Hebrews 11:1). It is as simple as that. You would think it unnecessary to further explain this simple and self-explanatory sentence. Unfortunately, in our lifetime we have seen war conducted in the name of faith, we have seen women young and old be beaten, tortured or killed in the name of faith. We have seen lands being burned and destroyed in the name of faith. We have seen discrimination, racial bias and hate crimes committed in the name of faith. Instead of empowering people to do good around them or aspire for greatness in life, faith has been turned into a weapon or a tool to crush people, their dreams or their lives.

In the early years when my story started airing in the media, I was interviewed by one journalist about my faith, or as she called it: "My claim that it is through faith that I have been able to overcome every challenge in life." Her question was: "If I am someone who believes in God, why do bad things keep on happening to me? Why does God let bad things happen to me?"

I had so many ways of answering that question that it was hard for me to choose the most relevant answer. So I just said, "Where should I start? Bad things shouldn't and don't happen to me or other people to test the power of God, the will of God or the love of God for us. There is nowhere in the Bible where it is said that we will never go through bad things or tragedies. On the contrary, every chapter in the Bible is about warning us against the bad things of life, but also teaching us ways to handle them. The problem with us is not the love of God, or the plan that God has for us. Instead the problem lies with the minds of humans. Because often our minds have been corrupted with all kinds of things, we start hearing the words differently, and we start trying to give our own meanings to the simple words we hear. By adding our own twists, spins or interpretations to suit us, we take those simple words or instructions to a whole new level or direction. When the Bible says, "You shall not steal," how simpler could that sentence be for people to understand what it says: don't take what is not yours without explicit permission. When the Bible says, "Respect your parents," it's just the same thing. These are very simple instructions, given in a direct language. But now if we start walking through library aisles, we see so many interpretations of these simple statements. There are so many different explanations on the conditions, the environment, the reasons and the levels. All these explanations try to make it okay to lie or steal, and as a result, we end up with different truths. People tend to choose what suits them, and the confusion over what is true or not true becomes an excuse for people to deviate from the original instruction of: "You shall not steal".

Knowing that most of our actions are guided by what we

believe our truth is, we get what we have nowadays in our society with people who can rape a woman they claim they love, people who kill others with no regards for human life; and yes, a man who can rob his own child from the peace and serenity that a warm, loving home provides to a newborn. Then we turn around and blame God for this, or ask why God is allowing this to happen. God gave us life, but he never promised to come live it for us.

I was at a funeral and the minister was preaching on the relationship between God and us, particularly what we do with the abundant love that God gave us and promised to sustain forever. He singled out the Garden of Eden parable as stated in Genesis chapter three. He called it: "Your life, your choice. But you will have to face the consequences of your decision." He explained that the problem with human beings is that we want everything but we don't want to be held responsible for what goes wrong with it. Then when something doesn't go our way, we blame God for allowing bad things to happen to us. He said that God created us simple, and gave us everything we should ever need in life. He made it available in the Garden of Eden. He told us that he created us to His image. He loved us so much that he put everything imaginable at our disposal: Good life, good health, wealth, food, joy, and everything that is good on earth. We were supposed to live a bright life surrounded with love, peace, prosperity and freedom. We even had the freedom to choose to live a life fulfilled with whatever we wanted. Nothing else was going to be above us or against us. All He asked was that a tiny, useless and irrelevant tree that he left standing somewhere there in the middle of that endless garden be left alone.

He warned that the tree in question produces a very dangerous and deadly fruit. He clearly stated that it would be our peril to touch it or consume it, and confessed to us that he doesn't want to see us harmed in any way, shape or form. So He begged us to stay away from the fruit of that insignificant tree. But did we listen? Of course not! So here we are supposed to be enjoying everything that is pure, rich, good, meaningful, fulfilling and worthy. We will grow wealthy, live long and have happiness for eternity. Instead, our mind became focused on that one little thing that we weren't supposed to touch, that is way beneath us, and what we were warned was hazardous to us. We were told it would cost us everything good that was already given to us. But that ugly, worthless, poisonous little fruit from that tree became the one thing we had to pursue. Forgetting the warning that said: "Eating it may mean death, touching it may mean destruction," we couldn't hear the voice that reminded us to be careful, to think it through, to wait another day before we make a final decision, to remember the original plan, to double check before we accept. When we eat the fruit and get poisoned or die, we blame God and curse God, and complain that he doesn't love us. God didn't do this to us, we did this to ourselves.

This is a great reminder of the fact that sometimes the hardships we go through are a consequence of a choice we made at one point in our life. It doesn't mean that we have to condone people who hurt others or take advantage of vulnerable people; nor does it mean that victims are asked to be hurt or taken advantage of. It just means that the choices we made of getting involved with certain people or being at certain places or doing certain things—directly or indirectly have an impact on the results we get. Sometimes we make choices with the best of our knowledge or intentions; and nevertheless, they turn out to be bad choices or mistakes. When the result is terrible, we shouldn't become more victimized by beating ourselves up over the choices we made. The important thing is to acknowledge the mistake and take steps to correct the situation and move on with our life.

Faith is what gives you the necessary humility to make that

difference. It's really not about placing blame. It's more about correcting the wrongs or the mistakes to allow yourself to move forward. You are in the journey of living life in a fulfilling way. Therefore, you have to be able to identify where the mistake was and set yourself up better to prevent making the same mistake in the future. But it's not always possible to have that ability because sometimes people's beliefs get in the way. In the same manner, our truth is derived from our beliefs, so are our beliefs equally derived from where or how our faith was born or instilled in us.

Faith can help or hinder us depending on how we understand it and where we got it from

I grew up in a very religious family where the entire extended family had to wake up at five in the morning every day to read a scripture and pray. We had to take turns in praying because it was extremely important for children and adults to get trained in the practice of praying, among other things. It didn't matter when you went to bed. Everybody had to be there with no exception every single day except Sunday, because it was church day. So if you went out the night before, you had to be back before we sat down to pray. Nobody was allowed to be missing unless they were out of town. It was a ritual, a routine life we were all engaging in without really understanding the true meaning of it all. Now a lot of people grow up that way and incorporate the habit in their life for many generations, but this practice has to be separated from living by faith.

I was twelve years old when I heard the most profound sermon from a local pastor who awakened my faith. I went to church that day because it was a special occasion where once a year all local pastors were invited to our church. It was like the annual big evangelical event, a preaching festival. Different choirs competed, and different pastors preached for the whole weekend. This wasn't my first time at this event as my parents brought me there every year, and I went there with the intention of enjoying the show and the competition like all the previous years. We were into the second day of the festival, hearing the different sermons, when a guest pastor took his turn on the podium and started talking about our freedom in life and how everything has a consequence. He said, "As the Bible tells us, '*Everything is permissible, but not everything is beneficial. Everything is permissible, but not everything is constructive. Nobody should seek his own good, but the good of others....*'" I learned later that it is from 1 Corinthians 10:23–24. Then he proceeded to read the scriptures of 2 Timothy chapters 1 and 2, and he read another passage about faith, comfort and compassion from 2 Corinthians 1:3–7, which says:

Praise be to God and Father of our Lord Jesus Christ, the Father of compassion and the God of all comfort, who comforts us in all our troubles, so that we can comfort those in any trouble with the comfort we ourselves have received from God. For just as the sufferings of Christ flow over into our lives, so also through Christ our comfort overflows. If we are distressed, it is for your comfort and salvation; if we are comforted, it is for your comfort, which produces in you patient endurance of the same sufferings we suffer. And our hope for you is firm, because we know that just as you share in our sufferings, so also you share in our comfort.

His voice alone was so powerful and so deep that at times it seemed to me as if he could speak to the crowd of more than a thousand people, without a microphone. Maybe it was just because I was captivated by what I was hearing. Later in closing with his sermon, he spent a lot of time on these lines:

For this reason I remind you to fan into flame the gift of God, which is in you through the laying on of my hands. For God did not give us a spirit of timidity, but a spirit of power, of love and of self-discipline.

It's amazing how he talked for two hours saying so many things. On top of the conviction that I would absolutely name my first two daughters Lois and Eunice; what I got from that preaching that day was that we have to be proud to be called "Children of God". If we stay strong, we stay courageous in the eyes of God, then we will always finish with victory. I understood that the efforts of my parents to sew faith into their children, is a great inspiration and gift for me to pass on to my children one day. I learned that day how people can go through problems in life, but every time, if we remember the power within us that God gave us, we shall be okay. That's the first time I understood that God loves us no matter what.

Then in the middle of the speech, the pastor said the most amazing thing. He said that faith is not about going to church every Sunday, dressed up nice, or singing in a choir. Faith is about what you do with your life every day that is good for you and others according to God's instructions and purpose. You have to put your heart to do good and be good. You have to put your mind to think good and do good. And you have to use your actions to do good and bring good in other people's lives. My faith was born right there and then at twelve years old. This even helped me better understand what my parents were teaching me. My dad was reminding us all the time to be responsible and act with integrity. I never knew what that meant until that sermon. My mom was insisting on generosity, kindness and uplifting others. I finally understood what it meant after that sermon.

Faith to me is not about blind hope and expectation. We know the story of a guy who was laying down on his bed every day saying, "God, please make me win the lottery, please make me win the lottery." After a year, God got fed up with his prayers and expectation, and finally responded to him: "Well, at least by a ticket". Faith is that unshaken belief and conviction that no matter what, the next day will be better. But you have to initiate the actions in the right direction.

Now to come back to the reporter who was asking me why God allowed bad things to happen to me, I could easily say that it was to allow me to figure out that I am actually even stronger than I thought. Every time we face a difficult moment, we are so quick to claim "Oh my god! This is the worst thing I have ever been through". Interesting enough, the next time we face another hard time, we say that is the worst thing we have ever been through. We keep saying that without realizing that our assessment of the ordeal is not really empowering because we have probably solved the issue; and in reality, it wasn't really that bad. You have to learn your own strength in order to build the necessary confidence that you can achieve big things; that you can build greatness, and you can go far beyond anything you ever imagined possible.

Faith is the force that should sustain us while we encounter trials and tribulations, if we want to use faith that way. Unfortunately there are two types of faith users: Those who use faith to justify their excuses to miss an opportunity, to fail or to harm; and those who use faith to empower themselves. Everyone makes the choice that suits them. From the Bible to the Koran, I am sure you can find a passage to justify anything you do, say or think. If you want to cheat, lie, steal or kill, the Old Testament will give you so much scripture that you wouldn't even know which one to use. If that is what we want to use faith for to get out of a situation, we will certainly be served.

So yes, we have the freedom to believe whatever we want,

but we also have to be very careful what we tell ourselves in the name of faith.

True faith lies in the power to overcome

We go through life facing a lot of things. We go to church and have been taught to believe in a higher power, call it whatever you want. I believe in God. Most people go through life without real struggles. They're the lucky ones. I sincerely believe that after all the discussions about what is faith, truth and reality are irrelevant. Everyone has a version of what faith, truth or reality means for them, which suits them. God will have the ultimate verdict, and so it is a total waste of time and a big distraction to engage in an ideological or philosophical discussion on this matter, especially when we have to face adversity, obstacles, doubt, enemies, uncertainty, disappointment, deception, and many other harmful or malicious situations.

When in trouble, what most people are looking for are solutions to their problems, or ways to improve their lives. From that point only, my opinion is very simple on the matter of what faith should be about. If I go back to the basic definition of faith as "being sure of what we hope for and certain of what we do not see," then faith has nothing to do with going to church any more than it has to do with trying to guess what God thinks. Faith has to be that tool we should use to empower ourselves. "For God did not give us a spirit of timidity, but a spirit of power, of love and of self-discipline." This is how I know that we can overcome even the impossible. Courage, resilience and tenacity come from that belief. So if you have that belief in yourself, nothing can stop you from moving forward.

True faith lies in the power that our belief procures us to fight when we face adversity, to resist when we face temptations, to not give up when we face obstacles, to find the courage to move forward when everything seems hopeless, and to force a crack or a hole when all doors seem closed around us. I've always said that faith to me has to be that unshakable belief that no matter what, there is a way out. When all doors seem closed around us and there appears to be no way out, we don't need to focus on breaking a wall. We don't need to start forcing the door to open. All we need is a tiny hole; and if a needle or an ant can go through it, we have to know that we can if we just start there.

Call it karma, luck, or whatever you like, but I call it the power of God at work: the unshakable belief that my life has a greater purpose than whatever obstacle I am facing at that moment. As long as I am still breathing and thinking clearly, there is a way forward.

Timothy 2:1, "But join with me in suffering for the gospel, by the power of God, who has saved us and called us to a holy life, not because of anything we have done but because of his own purpose and grace".

This is the belief I've carried since hearing that sermon at age twelve. I have carried it all my life, and I completely lived it at that shelter. Here we were, about fifty women in a shelter. We all shared the despair and hopelessness that comes with that situation, and I found a book in the dusty study of that shelter that helped me start my business and land my first contract while being homeless. I then proceeded in launching the most innovative service that has helped thousands of people find work, and inspired dozens of different business models across the planet offering these services.

Who am I to have such an impact?

I am just a woman from the tiny unknown village of Makak in southern Cameroon. My dad was a teacher all his life, and my mom was a stay-at-home mom all her life. My family was financially poor but spiritually strong and rich. I have no connections, and I don't have friends in high places. I am a complete nobody in a country or society where, if anything happens to me, you will barely find ten people that would be touched or affected by my misfortune. For all intents and purposes, at the moment when I made the gutsy move to start my business, not knowing what my tomorrow was going to be about, I was just destined to confirm the statistics of a black woman with her immigration status in limbo, getting involved with a man with questionable morals. "He cheated on her, lied to her and got her pregnant; then left her on the street with nothing but her baby!" What was ahead for me? Social assistance? prostitution? low-paying jobs? food bank…. But I had the resolve that this would not be me. I was still breathing, walking, talking and thinking. I still had everything that matters. The rest was up to me.

I never forgot that my mom told me I was born to do great things. But what I was going through and where my life seemed to be heading, contradicted every part of her statement. I was determined more than ever to find a crack on the wall of my prison and get out. I always believed that behind any closed door or brick wall that is keeping you inside a locked space, the rest of the world is waiting for you to enjoy it. No matter how deep or hopeless everything looks at that moment, it really is just a feeling. If you keep looking, there is always a better way. I might have been sitting in a shelter, everything might have looked doomed, I might be visibly confirming the statistics at that moment—but this is not me. There has to be a way.

I had my special prayer I had developed for myself when I was young, and it had stayed with me all my life. It's a mix of different biblical verses to suit my needs, and has carried me through every struggle, every obstacle, every adversity. And I know my will and confidence get solidified every morning after I read this:

I am more than conqueror.

My foes all whisper against me; they imagine the worst about me: I have a deadly disease, they say; I will never rise from my sickbed; I will never rise from the bottom of this pit hole I find myself in. Even the friends or people who had my trust, who shared my table, who shared my house, have scorned me. But you, LORD, have mercy and raise me up that I may repay them as they deserve by my rising right back up. By this I know you are pleased with me, that my enemy no longer jeers at me. For my integrity you have supported me and let me stand in your presence forever. Blessed be the LORD, the God all mighty, from all eternity and forever. The LORD's face is against evildoers to wipe out their memory from the earth. When the just cry out, the LORD hears and rescues them from all distress. The LORD is close to the broken hearted, saves those whose spirit is crushed. Many are the troubles of the just, but the LORD delivers from them all. God watches over all their bones; not a one shall be broken. Evil will slay the wicked; those who hate the just are condemned. The LORD redeems loyal servants; no one is condemned whose refuge is God. You are my help and deliverer; my God, do not delay! Lead me through the rocks that are higher than I. I fear no harm for you are at my side. You set a table before me as my enemies watch. Only goodness and love will pursue me all the days of my life. I will dwell in your house, O LORD for years to come.

They may laugh or dwell in my demises, they think they have won. They can gloat in their confused foolishness, because they don't understand and will never get it. The truth is: it was not really them but YOU God who had me come here for your greater purpose for me. Only your will should be done on your humble servant that I am in the name of Jesus. Amen.

Once I reminded myself of this fact, I never looked back. God had his purpose for me. I had these little contracts that allowed me to have enough money to move to my one-bedroom apartment. While I was finalizing my business plan, I uncovered the most amazing reality and niche market within the recruitment industry.

Grabbing each opportunity

I always dreamed of running my own business ever since I was a little girl. At six, I was selling candies, boiled eggs, donuts that my mom made, and peanuts. Once I became a teenager, I graduated to another level of products I could sell. My dad appointed me his assistant store manager at the local convenience store. I was also in charge of making a deposit at the post office where he had an account. He added a bar to the store, and he put me in charge of that division, managing inventories, orders and deliveries.

When I came to Canada, I knew I had to stand out and break through the cycle of newcomers who have to wait for more than ten years to make it. When I was told that volunteering is extremely valued in Canada, that it is considered as work, this was music to my ears. I just jumped on the opportunity to do what I really wanted and get involved in places where I could learn something in return. I found a spot at a radio station where I could help them with information on anything French and African; and in return they agreed to teach me how to produce a radio show from a technical level. After just one year volunteering and training, I heard there was an opening for a show on Wednesdays at noon. It was a timeslot that most people didn't want because they thought no one was listening to the radio at noon. Most people are at work at that time, thus they can't tune in. This was my chance to make my mark and land a radio show. I crafted a talk radio program focused on community affairs and promoting the French-speaking population that existed under the radar. Since it was the only program in French at the English radio station, I knew I had a catchy formula to draw attention to the program. But that wasn't enough. I selected a very lively jingle for the show that was a jazz piece from the late Michel Petrucciani, entitled "Looking Up". I knew I had an amazing attention-grabbing combination that would draw people to a noon radio program. The rest would just be the calibre of guests I would be able to attract.

After just two airings of the show, the phone kept ringing with inquiries on the music I was playing. Three months later, the main national radio station wanted to use that music for their report, and I started getting calls from public relations firms offering that I interview their clients, ranging from communication directors to university lecturers. I was booked every weekend to emcee an event somewhere in the city, and negotiated with the station to allow me to own my show and produce it myself. Even though this was a community radio station, I could see great potential, and for that reason I needed to have full control over my program. They gave me some conditions, and we were able to work out a deal. After making that radio program successful and having put myself on the map, I started dreaming of a production company. I had this big plan of producing shows and media pieces and of one day producing documentaries as I was coming across so many untold stories while doing my radio show. I planned to grow this company into a big consulting firm.

I had everything planned and ready. I had picked the name of the company, and the money I was saving while pregnant would be invested in the company very soon. Everything was prepared, and the third empty room in my house would serve as my home office. I ordered a separate phone line, set up a computer and all the necessary furniture, supplies and stationary. I had everything scheduled, and would take care of myself until I had the baby, and then use my maternity leave to rest and work on my business plan and getting more clients. The plan was to start looking for clients on a part-time basis, and keep saving money until I got to the point where I could launch that big company.

When my life fell apart and I ended up homeless and penniless, that dream was gone as well. Everything looked too complicated to contemplate a business any longer. How could I? I didn't even know where or when I would find a place to live that was stable enough to allow me to explore a business idea. I didn't know how long it would take for me to be in a position to save even a single dime, let alone enough money to support any business start-up. It takes a lot of time to concentrate and develop a business plan, then implement it or launch the business. When would I ever find the time? As far as I was concerned, that dream of starting a company was dead for now.

Sitting at that shelter every day, all I could do was to drown my sorrow. I watched the television until my head hurt. Time seems to stop when you have nothing to do, and I needed something to occupy my head, to shift my thoughts, and to get my mind out of my situation. I was struggling with my feelings and my mind, and knew that if I didn't nurture my mind fast enough, I would dwell over why I was there in the first place. That was the last thing I wanted to be putting my mind into. I wanted to think of how I could get out of there, and focus on getting on with my life.

There were rules in the house, such as a curfew at nine in the

Going from Homeless to CEO

evening, where nobody is allowed in after that time no matter what. You can't sleep in the rooms during the day, so you have to hold your baby when they sleep. Everyone has to do chores, and people take turns so it's not the same people who do the laundry or cook or clean all the time. I confided in the social worker that came twice a week how I was breastfeeding a hundred percent, and I really needed just a little calm sometimes. There was too much arguing and shouting in the television room, and I was literally going crazy, which can't be good for my baby. She suggested that if I wanted to isolate myself sometimes, there is actually a little room at the corner by the entrance. No one ever goes there because there are only books in there. I was stunned: "There are books in this place? There have been books in this place all this time, and I have been losing my mind slowly in here?"

The first day I just went there to sit down alone, breastfeed my baby and steal a few minutes of sleep if I could manage it. I didn't know what to expect from the books. Everything was seriously covered in dust. Two half-empty boxes were sitting there, and I could see some old brochures from the '80s about violence against women. I asked that my name be put down on the chore list for that room, and I offered to clean it. Frankly, my intention at that point was just to keep using that space for some alone time. When I started cleaning the room, I was amazed at the type of books that were buried in the dust: great reports on women's issues, studies on city policies and how they affect women, and all kinds of guides for women. It was an amazing treasure to me that was making me love that little place more and more. I started going there every day to read whatever book I found, and I was learning so much about women's issues, research conducted on families, the city, the province and its communities. Then came a one-of-a-kind discovery. I found a guide to planning and starting a small business as a low-income woman. It looked like a manuscript printed on one side of a regular page, and stapled on the side, with only one cover left on it. The information seemed to have been put together by a young researcher or a college student, and wasn't very sophisticated. It was written in a simple format, with words that didn't require a dictionary to comprehend. The chapters were short, and all the steps were defined with examples and little exercises to help the reader apply the lesson on that page. Well, I thought since I had nothing to do, and I had finished cleaning the room, I was going to occupy my time and my mind by following the steps suggested in the manuscript. I wanted to play along. Let's say that I want to start a business idea and create some revenue for myself. How would this work? At that point, I was not even thinking about planning the company I wanted to launch, I just wanted to have some fun with this book I had found, and keep myself busy while I was in the shelter.

The first lesson in the book was about knowing yourself. I had to make a long list of what I knew I could do, then break it down into categories from what might generate money for me now, and what may require more training, investment or expenses later on.

Another lesson was to make a list of who would be interested in the talent, skills or services I can offer. Then I was instructed to separate my list into those that I already know, and the rest that I don't know. The other lessons worked me through the process of contacting the potential clients to offer my talent, skills or services.

I went through all the steps, and to my great amazement, I had a viable business idea in my hands and a concrete possibility to start making money right there from that shelter where I had been desperately sitting for weeks, completely lost in myself, not knowing about my tomorrow. I decided to put the whole thing to the test, and I made my first phone call to a women's group that needed someone to help coordinate a one-day conference. After just forty-eight hours, I got the contract, and it was agreed that I would be paid five thousand dollars. Everything was done, and no one suspected that I was coming from a shelter. I completed the conference and finished a report for them from the shelter. Afterwards, I proceeded in calling other prospective clients, and a business was born. Everything I am today started in that dusty little room in the women's shelter.

Once out of the shelter and well settled in my apartment, I moved quickly to my next big idea: magazine publishing. While I was conducting a market research for that idea, I found out that although the idea was marketable, I wouldn't have been able to finance it. I concluded that it wasn't viable. But in the meantime, I gathered a lot of data and information that led me to the most exciting business idea. My educational background was in human resources and business administration, but I was never interested in placement agencies. I love communication, media, publishing, dealing with people and development. From my data collected, I noticed that the need for bilingual personnel was growing at a faster pace than even technology. I had to be creative in setting services that wouldn't compete with placement agencies and employment services at the community level, which catered to human resources managers in all companies and all sectors. I had to draw from my skills and knowledge to do all that. But I still had no money.

I came up with an idea to offer tools that can connect bilingual job seekers with employers, and I started by producing an employment newspaper that only displayed job ads and career tips or advice. I didn't know a single thing about publishing a newspaper, and I decided to be open about this fact with the printing company. They were kind enough to teach me the basics in one afternoon. Then I decided to test the market. I sent out a one-page survey to companies just asking if they were interested in advertising in such a newspaper. To my shock, four companies sent me ads and wanted me to get back to them with a quote. I didn't know what to do, so I called three different newspapers and asked if they would be willing to show me how a rate card should be done, or teach me how to price ads. Two sent me off, but a third one said they could help me, and they did. With four ads in my hands, which could produce enough money to cover the cost of printing the first issue, my only thought was: What am I waiting for? I called two services and requested their permission to display their information for free, and proceeded to publish my first newspaper. It only had four pages, but what pride I had. I never looked back, and kept on moving forward. The service grew to four other tools, with the result that over fifty thousand people have found work through my services.

The model that I initiated was so creative that dozens of similar models have since been implemented throughout the country, and the world. My only mistake was that I didn't trademark the model early on. But the impact has been tremendous and stemmed from an idea born from sitting in a dusty room of a homeless women's shelter.

CHAPTER 8

Setting up a residual income can be easier than you think

FOR THE PAST 10 YEARS, I HAVE BEEN TREMENDOUSLY BLESSED with the opportunity to teach at seminars about starting a business as a viable career option for women and immigrants. I have seen incredible women in need, with so much potential and so many bright ideas. It has been a great joy to see them make the choices that improved their lives and the future of their families. Knowing that I was part of that process fills my heart with gratitude.

Here are two examples among the dozens of ideas I have shared with my participants in the past few years to help them see how they too can take a simple idea and turn it into residual income, or create a serious revenue stream for themselves.

Baby delivery assistant/buddy

Maureen was a public health nurse who was counselling women at an abuse centre. She has seen all kinds of victims, all kinds of needs, and all kinds of solitude, despair and loneliness. After ten years of service she became a program coordinator in the geriatric centre at her local hospital. She kept her attachment to her community because giving back was a commitment she had made to herself a long time ago when she was still a student at the local college. Soon enough, she set up a wellbeing and health promotion volunteer program at a women's centre where she came in once a month and talked to young women or teenagers about everything from healthy nutrition to makeup, dressing up well, cosmetics, or heavy health issues like mental health, and so much more. The program was very entertaining and educational enough that it became the busiest at the centre. Each month, more than two dozen women met and talked about their issues, and learned more about how to better care for themselves and share their concerns.

With that little program, Maureen promoted healthy living and open communication on women's health issues. After one year delivering this monthly get-together with women, she noticed that more and more women from the prenatal courses were joining her program. Some openly discussed their fear of giving birth, the loneliness of the delivery room, and their spouses or partners not being there for them. These were rather middle class women, some were professionals, and others were married to a professional with a solid income. Even with all the money in the world, the fear of first birth or even second birth was a huge issue.

To her surprise, Maureen was sitting at the back of the room one day after her presentation, and a 42-year-old participant with her first child due in a few weeks, came to her with a startling proposition. "I will pay you at least $35 per hour, or even a $100, to come be with me at the hospital while I am going through childbirth," she said. The woman had a husband, but she wanted a buddy, someone she knew she could count on who would know how to hold her hand, and who wasn't emotionally involved or attached to the event. She wanted someone who could be compassionate enough to sympathize with what she was going through and would understand her when she was being difficult, to encourage her when she needed it, to push her when she needed to be pushed, and to help her calm down.

At first Maureen was puzzled by the proposition as she never thought that women can be in a situation where they are willing to pay somebody while they have partners or husbands. The woman explained that she loves her husband and she knows he will be there, but she also knows he won't be there the way she will want him to be, and she won't be in a state of mind to explain to him what she needs, or fight with him over what she needs, and she doesn't want to end up holding this against him. So to avoid all that potential crisis, she would rather pay for someone who knows what's going on at that moment, so that everybody is happy at the end.

Well Maureen said yes, and they had to just settle the fee and the payment scheme:

- If the delivery lasts for less than 24 hours, an hourly fee will be applicable.

- If the delivery goes over 24 hours, a flat fee of $600 per day will apply.

After that first experience, Maureen quickly realized that she had a special niche. While she was at the hospital helping her first client, she noticed how many other women could use such assistance. These are both younger and older women, some with their husbands or partners falling asleep while the woman is going through the pain of labour; and there are also the lonely nights when their partner or husband goes off to watch TV. Some women even reported having their men walk out and leave them in the hospital.

Maureen developed a one-page flyer that she posted on pre-natal class notice boards, as well as some other women's clubs, doctors offices, etc. Before she knew it, she was overbooked.

Dance classes

I came across Anna's salsa classes one summer while I was surfing the Internet looking for some evening clubs where I could go and practice my Latin dance. A friend had told me before that a lot of dance clubs in town offer free lessons, and they practice on weekdays.

I found a one-page website advertising salsa lessons. I called immediately, and a lady answered the phone telling me that her name is Anna. She explained that the intermediate and advanced classes have fifteen people presently enrolled in them, and she runs this class in four different locations in the city. I asked her if she is a professional dancer and if she comes from Latin America. She said, "None of that. I just know how to dance this style, and I enjoy teaching, so I figured why not share my knowledge with people who want to learn. I work full-time in a company as an account payable clerk." She made over $13,000 per month through her dance classes.

CHAPTER 9

Making success possible
no matter what

SUCCESS IS NOT NECESSARILY ABOUT BEING FAMOUS AND wealthy. We are successful every day in our own way and in our own lives. You can thrive for success no matter where you are or what circumstances you find yourself in. If we consider success as it is commonly defined—as the achievement of something desired, planned or attempted—then we should all feel successful every day. All you have to do is determine a goal and achieve it, and you are successful. Some people are successful for simple little things like getting out of bed in the morning. Therefore if you didn't fail, you have succeeded. Knowing this fact, why more people don't feel successful is beyond comprehension. We easily feel like failures because we don't learn the practice of counting our blessings and celebrating our accomplishments.

Success is the ability to see opportunity when it presents it-self. It's the art of seizing that opportunity, and it's the commitment to make it happen for you. All this can only be possible when someone allows themselves to believe that it is possible to achieve what they want, and that it's possible to have a better result. You have to want things to be better, to get better, to finish what you start or to accomplish what you set your mind to. Until you get to the state of mind where things have to change for you, you won't be able to bring yourself to make things happen for you. You won't be able to recognize an opportunity that can help you achieve what you want or get what you need, even when you are swimming in the opportunity day and night. Blindness is a terrible impairment that can sometimes be mental, and which is sometimes in all of us.

People tend to be easily contented with their circumstances and situations. You have to want to trigger the process of achievement. It is not enough to want something—you have to want something different, something new, a change from your usual circumstance, a change that can produce a different outcome, a bigger outcome with more satisfaction for it to count as a success.

The need to have a challenging situation doesn't necessarily mean that you have to create a crisis for yourself, or create a tragedy to overcome. It can simply be a goal you want to achieve or a vision you want to turn into reality. Thriving for success is thriving to make possibility into reality. It is turning opportunity into reality, and it is very fulfilling to achieve the goal you were aiming for or to get the result you were looking for. Of course, all of this is impossible if you don't need better things for yourself.

You have to want better for yourself

I don't believe that some people were born to be ambitious while some others were born to live mediocre lives. The same way, I don't believe that some are born good and others are born criminals. I firmly believe that we are all human beings capable of everything. The difference is just how the different stages of life ends up shaping us.

We become completely transformed through the abilities we acquire or develop based on the environment we are immersed into, where we have our interactions, and the training we receive, whether they are academic, spiritual or social experiences. You can't develop personally, professionally or socially if you don't want better for yourself. It is funny how babies understand this idea better than adults. At six months they are eager to move like all the other people they see around them, so they usually start pushing their bodies forward, and they end up crawling. Then they want to walk like all the other people they see around them, and before you know it they are holding onto everything they see around them. Babies understand that the first step in walking is to stand up then move their legs. They understand a process naturally, but a lot of adults don't. Babies can see that there is something better out there than what they're doing, and they absolutely want to be that and have that.

Sometimes in the darkest days of your life lies the beginning of the biggest story of your life. We get handed the key to our prosperity, healing, happiness, success or improvement; a unique opportunity that can shift our bad situation into a winning moment. The cruellest experience you can encounter might also be the exact moment when you find your greatest inspiration in life. Why do most people not even see the key? They are often too preoccupied by the negatives in their lives, the shortcomings, the regrets, the revenge, the resentment, the bitterness or the hurt.

Your worst nightmare can be the best chance for a greater life. I often say to everybody that my life actually started when I had my child and when I ended up homeless. A shelter is a blessing for any woman who is on the street. But don't get me wrong, it's nevertheless a very scary place because you are mixed with all kinds of people behaving and reacting strangely and unpredictably. You have heavy smokers, you have heavy drinkers, you can have what I call the social fighter: those women ready to be in your face for just looking at them, or not looking at them. This is not a sisterhood of the wounded or a sorority of sorts where, just because we have one thing in common, we are all the same. Don't expect everybody to be nice to you, to have compassion for you or empathy towards you. Someone can snap at you or turn against you at any time, and people are intense all the time. Then you also have the nice ones, those who will gladly watch your baby for you if you need two minutes, and those who will make sure that your baby is safe and entertained in order for you to catch a break. Some will offer to listen to you whenever you need to talk to someone who might understand what you are going through.

How often do we let opportunities pass by us and not grab them because grabbing them will require us to get outside our comfort zone, or because pursuing them will require us to completely turn 180 degrees on what we have known as a comfortable life up to that moment? Until you allow yourself to jump or to grab that opportunity, great success can't be achieved.

Be ready to see a life-changing opportunity whenever you are handed one. The world today belongs to people who seize opportunities whenever they present themselves. It is always hard to seize something you don't see. To be able to see, your mind has to be free of bitterness, resentment, self-pity, and all the other negative emotions that usually strip people from the power to move forward and achieve their best potential. I truly believe that life is a cycle. We are all supposed to end up happy, content and wealthy. The only thing that makes life worth living is the possibility of overcoming challenges, or the aspiration for a better tomorrow.